WASHINGTON'S
CHANNELED
SCABLANDS
GUIDE

WASHINGTON'S
CHANNELED
SCABLANDS
GUIDE

Explore and Recreate
along the Ice Age Floods
National Geologic Trail

John Soennichsen

THE MOUNTAINEERS BOOKS

THE MOUNTAINEERS BOOKS
is the nonprofit publishing arm of The Mountaineers,
an organization founded in 1906 and dedicated to the exploration,
preservation, and enjoyment of outdoor and wilderness areas.

1001 SW Klickitat Way, Suite 201, Seattle, WA 98134
© 2012 by John Soennichsen
All rights reserved
First edition, 2012
No part of this book may be reproduced in any form, or by any electronic, mechanical, or other means, without permission in writing from the publisher.
Distributed in the United Kingdom by Cordee, www.cordee.co.uk
Manufactured in the United States of America
Copy Editor: Kris Fulsaas
Cover, Book Design, and Layout: Emily Ford
Cartographer: Marge Mueller, Gray Mouse Graphics
All photography by author unless otherwise noted
Cover photograph: *A hiker peers out across the Channeled Scablands from the top of Steamboat Rock, Steamboat Rock State Park.* (©Alan Bauer)
Frontispiece: *Palouse Falls*

Library of Congress Cataloging-in-Publication Data

Soennichsen, John.
  Washington's Channeled Scablands guide : explore and recreate along the Ice Age Floods National Geologic Trail / by John Soennichsen.
    p. cm.
  ISBN 978-1-59485-483-5 (pbk.) — ISBN 978-1-59485-484-2 (ebook)
  1. Hiking—Washington (State)—Guidebooks. 2. Hiking—Ice Age Floods National Geologic Trail—Guidebooks. 3. Outdoor recreation—Washington (State)—Guidebooks. 4. Outdoor recreation—Ice Age Floods National Geologic Trail—Guidebooks. 5. Washington (State)—Guidebooks. 6. Ice Age Floods National Geologic Trail—Guidebooks. I. Title.
  GV199.42.W2S644 2012
  796.509797—dc23
                          2011042554

ISBN (paperback): 978-1-59485-483-5
ISBN (e-book): 978-1-59485-484-2

CONTENTS

INTRODUCTION

Back in the 1960s and '70s—during my teens and early twenties—I lived and worked in the Southern California suburbs of Los Angeles but spent every available weekend exploring Death Valley and other parts of the Mojave Desert. I regularly set out on hikes, four-wheel-drive excursions, and the occasional cliff scrambling junket, and I often encountered drivers who were passing through the area, generally on their way from point A to point B. As we were all filling up with gas or visiting a rest stop, they would see my backpack and hiking gear and ask me pointedly, "Just what is there about this godforsaken place that brings you way out here?"

"It's dry and dusty and hot and rocky," they would further enlighten me. "In fact, there's just nothing out here."

"Exactly," I'd reply, "and the fact that there's nothing out here—the fact that this is wide-open country with few people, fewer roads, and hardly a sign of modern civilization—is exactly what attracts me to the desert."

Of course, there was more to it than that. I loved to gaze out at the towering brown mountains, hike through the narrow canyons, and scramble down into the rocky desert washes I found around nearly every bend of the road. The sand dunes and salt flats and eroded buttes all seemed to call to me, and for a dozen years and more I set out to explore this dry and gravel-strewn terrain every chance I got.

Then, like some erratic rock, I was abruptly transported to the Pacific Northwest by a series of job changes and relocations—first to green and rainy Portland, where I pretty much figured my desert exploration days were over. Before long, however, I made another move—this time to the Spokane, Washington, area. Here, I learned that I now lived on "the dry side of the state," a region in direct conflict with most peoples' perceptions of Washington as a collection of fern-filled gullies, silvery waterfalls, snowcapped mountains, and large men in overalls tossing salmon around.

Little by little, I came to develop a newfound delight in my fresh surroundings. And as I began to explore the vicinity, I learned about the region's dramatic geological past, its one-of-a-kind scabland terrain, and

Previous page: *Twin Sisters, as seen from the "back side"*

its curiously desertlike environment—though the region is technically not a desert but a shrub-steppe plateau terrain.

The region in Washington State known as the Channeled Scablands is part of a much larger area, defined by a cataclysmic event that originated in western Montana. A massive flood of unimaginable proportions swept through northern Idaho, Washington, and Oregon, its waters extending as far south in the Willamette Valley as Eugene. The huge swath of interconnected geologic features created by this ice-age flood is now collectively referred to by some as the Ice-Age Flood Pathways. Part III of this book tells more of that larger story; in Part I, we take a closer look at Washington's portion of this massive terrain—and in Part II, you'll find details on exploring this fascinating area.

Exciting things are in store for the Channeled Scablands. Legislation creating an Ice Age Floods National Geologic Trail has recently passed, so there will soon be a wealth of maps, brochures, highway signs, information centers, and a network of suggested driving routes and hiking trails to help people experience a variety of routes and loop trips as they explore the scablands of eastern Washington, not to mention points east, west, north, and south. Visitor centers will eventually offer displays and programs explaining the monumental event that shaped this region's topography several thousand years ago. The wonderful geologic marvel that is the

Badlands area near Benton City

Beautiful Palouse Canyon

Channeled Scablands is the focus of the Ice Age Floods Institute, which has a role to play in the broader movement to establish the Ice Age Floods National Geologic Trail.

The Channeled Scablands is a place of dramatic geology: features such as massive coulees, abandoned waterfalls, narrow canyons, deep potholes, striking basalt buttes, and incredibly large boulders dramatically perched in the unlikeliest of places. Unlike many popular destinations with one prominent natural feature—a mountain, a canyon, a lake—dominating a fairly small area, Washington's scablands contain a variety of attractions spread out over a nearly 2,000-square-mile region of flood-sculpted terrain.

This vastness has both negative and positive consequences. First, because the scablands' many fascinating features are distributed over a broad swath of terrain, they can't all be incorporated into a single state park or national monument. On the positive side, the attractions worth seeing are ideally situated for visiting over a period of a few days or weeks, perhaps incorporating a few overnight camping experiences. In this book, I have also designed several loop trips that allow you to spend several hours driving to many scabland features and ending your day back where you began. Finally, if you're really pressed for time, a number of scabland sites lie not far from major roads and highways, which means they can be experienced briefly, even if you are merely passing through the region on your way from, say, Seattle to Spokane.

One benefit of the scablands' large geological footprint is that it allows visitors to choose among various modes of exploration. From hiking to biking to canoeing and kayaking, not to mention rock climbing and swimming, boating, and driving—the scablands can be explored in a variety of ways. What's more, those readers who are attuned to specific activities such as bird-watching, hiking, fishing, or hunting can enjoy these pursuits in a scabland setting where the scenery provides a striking backdrop.

Another great plus to the scablands' monumental expanse (in my mind, at least) is the sheer emptiness of it all, the relative lack of people to encounter as you explore the region's many attractions. To be sure, the more well-known this region's geologic features become, the more people there will be heading out to discover them. But as of early 2012, more than just a few spectacular geological attractions are still devoid of any directional signs, and in some areas you can spend an entire day on a trail without seeing another soul.

Just as I was able to escape urban Los Angeles now and then to seek solace in the Mojave Desert, the Channeled Scablands' wide-open expanses with few people, fewer roads, and hardly a sign of modern civilization might be just the restorative that city-dwellers from Seattle to Spokane—or anywhere else in the United States—are looking for.

Basalt cliffs in Moses Coulee

A NOTE ABOUT SAFETY

Safety is an important concern in all outdoor activities. No guidebook can alert you to every hazard or anticipate the limitations of every reader. Therefore, the descriptions of roads, trails, routes, and natural features in this book are not representations that a particular place or excursion will be safe for your party. When you follow any of the routes described in this book, you assume responsibility for your own safety. Under normal conditions, such excursions require the usual attention to traffic, road and trail conditions, weather, terrain, the capabilities of your party, and other factors. Because many of the lands in this book are subject to development and/or change of ownership, conditions may have changed since this book was written that make your use of some of these routes unwise. Always check for current conditions, obey posted private property signs, and avoid confrontations with property owners or managers. Keeping informed on current conditions and exercising common sense are the keys to a safe, enjoyable outing.

The Mountaineers Books

ACKNOWLEDGMENTS

Writing a guidebook was many times more difficult than I originally imagined. It's much more than just driving or hiking somewhere and then telling people how to get there and what they'll see. It's also not something done in isolation. Not all that long into the process, I became amazed at the numbers of people I was consulting, questioning, tagging along with, or asking for opinions. All of them were immeasurably helpful in many ways.

Thanks so much to geologist Bruce Bjornstad, for answering all sorts of questions I have posed over the past three or four years. The same goes for geologist Gene Kiver, who first got me interested in the scablands and who has always been available for questions or concerns.

A big thank-you goes to Randy Hill, wildlife biologist at Columbia National Wildlife Refuge, who gave me good advice about getting around in the mazelike terrain of the Drumheller Channels.

Thanks also go to Columbia Plateau Trail Ranger John Tillison, who took me on a personalized day-long guided tour of the trail from Cheney all the way to Benge. What a great day that was!

To all the helpful Bureau of Land Management folks who took time to meet with me and provide maps, directions, and advice, thank you all so very much! BLM personnel included Scott Pavey and Steve Smith with the Spokane office and Brent Cunderla and Kelly Courtright with the Wenatchee office.

My sincere appreciation to Ken and Susan Lacy, who let me stay over at their lovely Trinidad home and watch the elk cross the flood ripples at West Bar.

Thanks to Gracie Pena and all the rest of the weather team at KREM-2 TV in Spokane, for helping me to determine windows of opportunity when I could go out and get great photos. Thanks as well to Colby Newman with the National Weather Service, who told me how to use online weather maps to tell me where there was and wasn't snow-covered ground.

A million thanks to Kris Fulsaas, copy editor for this book, who couldn't have possibly devoted more time and care to this book had it been her own manuscript. And to Kate Rogers, editor-in-chief at The Mountaineers

Books, thanks so much for taking on this project and believing it could be a successful and popular guidebook. Senior Editor Mary Metz guided the book through its final stages before printing, and like the last steps of a long hike, the process left me feeling satisfied and with a definite sense of having accomplished something worthwhile. Thanks so much, Mary!

Lastly, my sincere thanks to my wife, Marilyn; daughter, Heidi; and sons Robby and Donny, who all took turns accompanying me when I headed out into the middle of nowhere to hike and observe and write and take photos, even though I sensed that their chief concern was to come along with me "so Dad doesn't get lost."

Opposite page: *Towell Falls at Escure Ranch*

PART I

The Channeled Scablands:
An Overview

ONE

THE SCABLANDS' GEOLOGIC PAST

Even if you're not a geology whiz, it's easy to see that the region referred to as the Columbia Plateau was the site of some bizarre geologic events in the distant past. The Channeled Scablands region exhibits a variety of strange and dramatic geological features caused by ice-age flooding some 15,000 to 18,000 years ago. As you explore this area, you'll encounter forest and farmland, lakes and streams—but the primary geologic player in evidence is basalt rock in a variety of forms. Coulees are lined with basalt columns; eroded plateaus of brown-black basalt thrust up above the surrounding soil to form buttes and tablelands reminiscent of the American Southwest. Scattered haphazardly throughout the scablands are weathered pieces of basalt—from softball-sized stones to chunks the size of school buses, as if they have been tossed around by some demented Goliath with rocks in his pockets.

Basalt is a form of lava that oozes out from beneath the earth's surface, then hardens as it cools and splits into multisided (often hexagonal) columns. As near as geologists can tell, the eruptions that caused this lava to seep out of the ground and cover the entire Columbia Plateau began about 17 million years ago. For 11 million years or so, there were continuing eruptive phases, divided by periods of calm. We can see evidence of these phases by observing the multiple "stacked" layers of basalt making up the towering walls of deep chasms such as Grand and Moses coulees.

When the periodic eruptions of lava ended—around 6 million years ago—the tops of the cooled layers of basalt rock were slowly covered by blowing silt over thousands of years. In areas where the silt collected in the deepest piles, dunelike hills were formed. The rich agricultural region we call the Palouse now occupies much of the southeastern corner of Washington along the Idaho border, but it is thought that such rolling hill country was once the dominant geologic feature from Spokane south to the Snake River and west all the way to the great bend of the Columbia River that divides Washington's eastern and central regions.

Today, as we gaze out over hundreds of square miles of broken basalt, deep potholes, dry channels, and exposed basalt columns, we likely are

Previous page: *The south alcove of Potholes Coulee*

seeing what was once an area of rolling hills, just as can be viewed today in the Palouse area around Colfax and Pullman. Where did all those other dunelike Palouse Hills go? Most geologists in the first few years of the twentieth century believed that glacial ice had moved south and carved away much of the soil of the scabland region, leaving behind only a few remnants of the hills that compose the Palouse area today.

One geologist, however, saw the signs of swiftly running water in those steeply sloped hills that remained. J Harlen Bretz (no period after the J, thank you) spent a decade in the 1920s trekking across the boot-gnawing terrain of the scablands. Even in his first year out here—1922—he noted that the north ends of all those Palouse Hills were steeper than the southern ends. To Bretz, this meant that water rushing at high speed from the north had eroded and steepened these northern slopes of the hills while also sheering soil off both side slopes until the hills resembled great islands of rich earth, surrounded by areas of scablands.

Bretz wrote a paper in 1923 that theorized a catastrophic flood arising from somewhere north of Spokane and surging across the Columbia Plateau at high speed, quickly excavating the coulees, deep potholes, dramatic waterfalls, and towering basalt cliffs that make up the scablands today.

By asserting such a hypothesis, Bretz became a pariah to other members of the geologic community, who preferred to envision scenarios of slow, gradual change over hundreds of thousands of years, not a short-lived flood that smacked of Biblical catastrophe. But Bretz was unwavering in his beliefs and eventually was proven to be correct some four decades later. A massive glacial lake in Montana was found to have been held in place by a monstrous glacial ice dam, and that dam had failed—not once, but many times, spilling out its contents over the landscape stretching southwest all the way to the Columbia River and then to the sea.

Ice played another part in the story, too: arms, or "lobes," of glacial ice extended all the way west to the Pacific Ocean and all the way east to the Atlantic. While the lobe of ice that blocked the Clark Fork River and formed Glacial Lake Missoula may have been the chief culprit in creating the subsequent Bretz floods (as they are now sometimes called), other lobes farther west periodically moved south and then retreated back north as the glacial

BRETZ'S CLUES

The first experience that J Harlen Bretz had with the Channeled Scablands was in the department of geology at the University of Washington back in 1911, when he saw a topographic map of Quincy Basin's Potholes Coulee. What Bretz saw in the closely spaced, concentric lines of that map were the dry remnants of a multitiered waterfall with some sections more than 400 feet high—in the middle of a desert. Later explorations led Bretz to conclude that the Glacial Lake Missoula floods had inundated Quincy Basin and filled it like some humungous bathtub until leaks developed at three low spots running north to south along the western edge of the basin. The middle of these three outlets was Potholes Coulee, where the rapidly flowing floodwaters carved two contiguous U-shaped alcoves lined with cataracts and separated by a peninsula of basalt about 1.5 miles long and 1,000 feet wide. After his first exposure to Potholes Coulee, Bretz began to see scabland features in a new, hugely expanded light.

ice ever so slowly waxed and waned like ocean tides. One of these arms of ice (today referred to as the Okanogan Lobe) is thought to have moved south and blocked the Columbia River a few times, diverting the river so it flowed down through what are now Moses and Grand coulees. And so, the story of the Channeled Scablands is a complex tale of ice and water, water and ice, a story that remained a mystery until first studied and revealed by J Harlen Bretz.

Like the blockbuster special effects of a major motion picture, the scablands of eastern Washington can be enjoyed and appreciated for their spectacular scenery even if you don't possess a full understanding of how they were formed. But those of us who are self-described geology junkies believe that a full understanding of what went on behind the scenes some 15,000 to 18,000 years ago can only enhance our enjoyment and appreciation of this unique region. The sections below provide some insights into the major features of the Channeled Scablands, but if you want more than a quick review of the geologic sequence of events that formed the Channeled Scablands, there are several good books and some DVDs that provide great computer animation of the colossal floods as geologists imagine they must have appeared (see Recommended Resources at the end of this book).

BASALT 101

Millions of years ago, much of the Pacific Northwest was inundated by repeated flows of lava emerging from beneath the earth, rising to the surface, then spreading out over the landscape, again and again. When each lava flow cooled into basalt, it formed many-sided columns of rock, which were eventually capped by the next flow of lava, then another, and so on. In some places, the multiple layers of basalt are 1,000 feet thick and more.

After all the lava flows had ended, blowing soils eventually covered the basalt rock, and over thousands of years a landscape was created across eastern Washington composed of rolling, grass-covered hills. Today, we call these the Palouse Hills.

When the ice-age floods swept through some 15,000 to 18,000 years ago, they washed away much of the overlying soils, exposing the basalt beneath. Then the basalt itself began to break apart at the joints between columns. The velocity and volume of floodwaters swept away the broken blocks of basalt, leaving coulees and canyons flanked by walls of columnar basalt that had been washed clean of the overlying soil.

Stacked basalt blocks along Columbia Plateau Trail

Basalt is common all around the Northwest. It can be beautiful in its geometrical perfection, and it also speaks of the tremendous forces that carved the landscape and scoured away much of the basalt rock underlying the landscape. One thing that all the features in the Channeled Scablands have in common is the underlying rock—basalt.

Basalt appears in a variety of column types, from sharp-edged, very symmetrical pillars to columns that look as though they were stacked together, one small section atop another. Some columns are straight as an arrow, while others weave and bend; all these variations are tied to the speed with which the lava cooled and the stability of the terrain over which the lava flowed. The age of the various flows also determines to some degree the color, hardness, and stability of individual basalt columns.

The presence or lack of groundwater can also affect the look of basalt. Pillow basalt, for example, which actually shapes itself something like a bed pillow, is the result of hot lava flowing where there was standing water. Pillow basalt can be seen near Vantage, Washington; in Moses Coulee; and at Sand Hills Coulee north and south of State Route 26 west of Washtucna.

Next time you take a drive in the scablands, keep a look out for basalt formations, including columns. They're all around us in the fascinating landscape of the Inland Northwest.

COULEES AND HOLLOWS AND DRAWS, OH MY!

Like many people new to eastern Washington—as I was a little more than twenty years ago—I didn't at first fully understand the meaning of the word "coulee." I later learned that the word comes from the French *couler*, which can mean "to flow," "to run," or "to sink." The context for which eastern Washington's flood channels are called coulees no doubt ties in best with the meaning "to sink," since coulees appear as fallen or sunken strips of land.

A coulee differs from a river valley in part by its generally U-shaped configuration, as opposed to the typical V-shape of a river valley. Also distinguishing a coulee from a river valley is the absence of a flowing creek or stream, although some former flood channels with modern streams in them are sometimes referred to as coulees. At the same time, a number of U-shaped gorges in eastern Washington *do* contain flowing water but are not called coulees.

Channel leading to Esquatzel Coulee

Wilson Creek and Canniwai Creek, for example—a pair of streams that meander across the Telford–Crab Creek Tract of the Channeled Scablands—flow through oversize, U-shaped canyons that could easily be called coulees but are not actually coulees. Other sunken areas of land, some with intermittent streams and others not, have been given colorful names including "draw," as in Gibson Draw north of Wilson Creek, or "hollow," as in Marlin Hollow north of Odessa. All these pathways represent existing stream or creek valleys that were dramatically expanded thousands of years ago when water from the Missoula floods found these valleys and dug them deeper as the water followed them to the Columbia River.

Whatever they're called, there is clearly a distinction between traditionally formed river valleys or canyons and those U-shaped channels that were formed—or, in some cases, expanded—by the force of swiftly flowing, incredibly deep floodwaters.

SCABLAND LAKES ARE DIFFERENT

I grew up believing that lakes are always found in pine-covered mountains, with towering, snowcapped peaks as a backdrop. A handful of cabins nestled beside the sandy shore, where a gently sloping, forested hillside met the peacefully lapping water.

Dry falls between Badger and Wiliams lakes

Years later, I saw my first scabland lake and realized I had led a sheltered life. To reach a scabland lake, a traveler does not ascend a looping roadway high up into the mountains. Generally, in fact, you're driving across a relatively flat landscape when it appears that the landscape is falling away in front of you. A canyon or gorge seems to lie ahead, and as you draw closer you see that the walls of this gorge are composed of black or brown basalt, often in dramatic vertical columns that plunge down to the surface of water below. The road to the lake drops and generally winds a bit as it negotiates the descent into a prominent gash in the earth before you.

Scabland lakes look the way they do because they were created by the massive flows of water that were the ice-age floods. Scabland lakes are *kolk* lakes, named after the violent, tornadolike underwater vortices found in major, fast-moving floodwaters. The depressions in which *kolk* lakes lie were formed by swirling water that plucked out basalt rocks to form a depression. In some cases, there might originally have been a stream or small valley, and this natural depression in the terrain attracted floodwaters in the first place as they sought lower ground in their rush from Montana to the sea. An existing valley or streambed, or even a fault-caused line of weakness in the underlying rock, was quickly exploited by the floodwaters. In the end, the floodwaters stripped an area of its protective soil and then its underlying basalt. What remained after the flood had ceased was a deep, narrow channel or coulee with towering basalt walls and a generally dry floor.

Over time, water tables rose and those dry floors became lakes. The reason the water in those lakes didn't simply run out was because the floods had carved deep plunge pools or potholes in the rocky floor beneath the surface of the water. The tornadolike action of the rapidly flowing water drilled out deep areas in these basins as they were being formed, and these holes captured and held water many thousands of years later. Some of these lakes have water sources from creeks and streams; others are fed only by rainwater or springs. Some of the lakes are alkaline because they are not regularly refreshed.

Floodwaters flowing across the scablands ran predominantly from northeast to southwest, so nearly all lakes in the scabland region are not only long and narrow but also oriented northeast to southwest. The lakes are generally situated in a canyon or gorge flanked by vertical basalt cliffs. Often these lakes are laid out in a chain, one lake followed by another, with a low marshy area or a dry fall (a long-abandoned waterfall) between them. At some scabland lakes, thousands of years after the last ice-age flood, you can stand at the top of a once-cascading waterfall and gaze

AN INTRODUCTION TO THE ICE-AGE FLOODS

The Ginkgo Petrified Forest State Park's visitor center just north of Vantage, although outside the boundaries of the Channeled Scablands, provides an excellent overview of the ice-age floods that erupted from Glacial Lake Missoula 15,000 to 18,000 years ago. If you are heading to the scablands from the Puget Sound region via Interstate 90, it's worth a brief side trip to view the short video and gaze at the excellent wall-sized map of the ice-age floods before you continue across the Columbia River into eastern Washington.

down at the abandoned plunge pool—normally a deep pool of water generally found at the base of an active waterfall. Sometimes these ancient plunge pools are just as dry as the falls; other times they are filled or partially filled with water.

Opposite page: *Pool at base of Dutch Henry Falls in Moses Coulee*

TWO

THE CHANNELED
SCABLANDS
ENVIRONMENT

The Channeled Scablands are spread out over nearly 2,000 square miles of eastern Washington, though more scabland terrain can be found in Oregon, mostly along the Columbia River. This chapter gives an overview of Washington's Channeled Scablands' environment, from climate, plants, and animals to human history both ancient and recent.

THE CLIMATE OF THE CHANNELED SCABLANDS

Among biologists who categorize the different ecosystems of various landforms—from coastal to alpine, desert to marshland—there is technically no such thing as a "scabland habitat" or ecosystem. The region as a whole is called the Columbia Plateau, although writer Jack Nisbit, in his book *Singing Grass, Burning Sage*, reveals the other names commonly associated with the region: Columbia Basin, Coulee Country, Sagebrush Country, the Scablands, the Big Bend, and, simply, the Dry Side.

Whatever you call it, the region encompassing the Channeled Scablands is considered a shrub-steppe environment—not a true desert, but sufficiently deficient in moisture that sagebrush is the dominant vegetation. Summers here are hot and dry; winters are cold and mostly dry. Precipitation falls chiefly between late fall and early spring. Annual averages differ depending where you are, from just 6 inches along the Columbia River near the Tri Cities to around 18 inches near Cheney, at the northeastern edge of the region. Snow falls in the scablands but rarely lasts long before melting. Temperatures in the Channeled Scablands can range from subzero in winter to more than 100 degrees Fahrenheit in summer, but the annual average is somewhere from the low 40s to mid-50s.

Humidity and rainfall in the scablands are sufficient to support smaller bushes, grasses, and flowers but only sparse clumps of trees and no true woodlands or forests, except for the pine forests in the northernmost reaches of the scablands. And yet, the biologically rich Columbia Plateau supports eighteen prevalent plant species and numerous endangered birds, among them the sharp-tailed grouse, the sage thrasher, and the sandhill crane.

Road through Telford Scabland in winter

PLANTS OF THE CHANNELED SCABLANDS

While sagebrush is part of an oft-used name for this region, the scablands are also home to a wide variety of other dry-land shrubs with unappealing names like bitterbrush and saltbrush. It is surprising to many visitors that plants with berries, including serviceberry and chokecherry, can be found in some scabland canyons and along the shadowy bases of basalt cliffs.

In spring, scabland panoramas are frequently decorated with the pastel hues of flowering, low-growing plants that provide a colorful contrast to a landscape that more often consists of varied shades of brown most of the year. Common flowers encountered along scabland trails include penstemons, balsamroots, sunflowers, lupines, larkspur, Indian paintbrushes, lomatiums, blue flax, pink phlox, lavender daggerpod, blue iris, and western gromwell, with its unusual pale green flowers.

Common in landscapes where basalt surfaces dominate are a wide variety of mosses, lichens, and algae. Tall, cracked, and weathered columns of dark basalt in Grand and Moses coulees are covered with colorful green, yellow, and orange lichens.

ANIMALS OF THE CHANNELED SCABLANDS

With such a varied community of plant life inhabiting the Columbia Plateau, there is an equally large community of tiny animal life inhabiting those plant environments. Stop for a moment along any hiking trail in the Channeled

Scablands and listen for the inevitable cacophony of hums, buzzes, chirps, clicks, and fluttering sounds, all generated by a vast squadron of flying, crawling, and leaping things.

Among the diverse and varied creatures that nest in, feed upon, and lay their eggs in vegetation of the scablands is a remarkably large number of insects. These include literally hundreds of different species of flies, beetles, bees, wasps, ants, and moths. Butterflies—more than 100 species of them—flit above the sage- and saltbrush on brightly colored wings of blue and yellow, orange and white.

Surprisingly, many species of insects depend on specific species of plants for their survival. The Indra swallowtail lays its eggs only on the leaves of desert parsley, for example, and the orange monarchs need clumps of milkweed to complete their breeding cycle. Sagebrush sheepmoths require—you guessed it—a landscape abundant in sage to feed on, mate in, and lay their eggs upon.

Like the myriad plants and insects inhabiting this region, the more than 27 species of reptiles and amphibians that are found here seek specific niches—some quite small—within the scabland environment. Amphibians, for example, search for the cool, damp, dark habitats provided by marshes, minigrottoes at the base of waterfalls, and damp crevices along the walls of basalt cliffs. Among the varieties of amphibians found throughout the Columbia Plateau are toads, frogs, and two species of salamanders.

Reptiles are represented by the western painted turtle, five species of lizards—including the western skink and the short-horned lizard—and nine varieties of snake, including our friend the rattler but also the striped whipsnake, the rubber boa, and the night snake, which is often mistaken for a young rattlesnake but is markedly different because its tail tapers to a point and has no rattles.

One warning you will probably receive from all seasoned scabland hikers who care to share a few words of wisdom is to watch out for rattlesnakes (see sidebar). Avoiding long hikes through tall brush and scabby basalt landscapes during the hot summer months is probably the best way to eliminate the threat of running into a rattler.

Among the most numerous of all creatures living in this region are its nearly 200 species of birds, from songbirds to water birds to raptors. Many

BRETZ'S CLUES

When Bretz first began his exploration of the great shiplike hills of Palouse soil found amid the dry, ragged channels of scabland, he noted that the "prows" of these ships always pointed north. This suggested to Bretz that they had been carved into their current shapes by large volumes of water flowing from north to south. Part of Bretz's closer examination of these "Palouse Islands," as he soon called them, involved the use of a simple kitchen colander to sift through the soil at various heights on the steep slopes facing scabland channels. Wherever he found coarse-grained basalt particles, he knew the floodwaters that carried these pebbles of basalt had reached each specific level on the hill where he stood. When he no longer found such particles, he knew he was standing above the level of the floodwaters. These measurements allowed him to get a better picture of the depth and width of individual channels of water.

are native, but others are merely stopping here to pass some time on their way north or south. Their presence is largely due to the many marshes, streams, lakes, and other wetlands that supply them with the food, water, and shelter they need. Songbirds you might encounter on a hike through the scablands include finches, wrens, robins, and meadowlarks.

Water birds range from the comical coot to a variety of ducks and geese to the white pelicans found in growing numbers throughout the Inland Northwest. Locations where such birds gather in large numbers include Turnbull National Wildlife Refuge, where bird-watchers also gather in large numbers to monitor the birds' activities (while the birds are no doubt observing the humans in similar fashion). In Columbia National Wildlife Refuge near Othello, thousands of people gather in February to watch the newly arrived sandhill cranes. From Harrington to Odessa, from Hog Lake to Jameson Lake, any place where bodies of water are found in this otherwise arid expanse of hot rock and dry sage, water birds will gather.

The more reclusive raptors in the scablands are warier of the humans who come to watch them through binoculars, but patience can be rewarded by spotting a vulture or falcon soaring above Coffeepot Lake, a rough-legged

Marmot family outing

hawk or pair of burrowing owls at Drumheller Channels, or a nesting bald eagle in Grand Coulee's Northrup Canyon area.

Mammals in the scablands are chiefly small in size, but incredibly active. Mice, rats, voles, marmots, and hares—including the rare pygmy rabbit—all are creatures of the night, foraging all night long and dozing in earthen tunnels during the hot summer days. In the winter, most of these animals hibernate underground. Muskrats and beavers live out their lives in the lands near lakes and marshes.

Larger mammals that actively patrol the scablands include badgers, bobcats, and coyotes. The largest residents of this region—all hoofed animals—range from mule deer to antelope to elk, and even the occasional bighorn sheep can be seen clattering among the rocks high on the slopes of taller buttes and basalt scarps overlooking the flood-ravaged lowlands.

While at first blush, you may set out on a desolate scabland trail feeling completely alone in utter solitude, it won't take long to realize you are surrounded by native communities of plants and animals that call this challenging terrain and region of eastern Washington their home.

EARLY HUMANS IN THE CHANNELED SCABLANDS

It's nearly impossible, while trudging up a trail through a ragged, basalt-strewn flood channel in the scablands, to *not* find yourself wondering how our ancient ancestors managed to live and survive here long ago in this harsh and otherworldly terrain. Just as fascinating is the exercise of speculating whether early humans could have lived here before the floods, perhaps even witnessing the arrival of these disastrous events on more than one occasion.

Anthropologists working in this region have failed to find any signs of people or their artifacts dating from a time before the floods. To some, this simply means that ancient tribes of nomadic people did not migrate to this region until after the last flood event had occurred, some 15,000 years ago.

But consider another, equally logical explanation: humans may well have been here before the floods, but their very traces of existence were obliterated, completely removed, by the floods. After all, where did most early peoples on Earth congregate and build their earliest shelters and encampments? *In lowland valleys, along streams and rivers.* And where did the floodwaters flow after Glacial Lake Missoula burst free of the ice dam that held it in place? Clearly, the floods followed just these lowland creases in the earth's surface, taking the most accessible and easily traversed paths to the Columbia River and then the Pacific Ocean.

We know that Native Americans from the Spokane tribe have an oral history that talks of great floods and changes in the landscape in and around the Spokane area. We know, too, that early humans inhabited the Channeled Scablands after the floods had passed. Spear points dating back approximately 11,000 years ago were found in East Wenatchee in 1987. At the Marmes Rock Shelter, near the mouth of the Palouse River where it joins the Snake, radiocarbon dating suggested habitation at this site as long as 13,000 years ago. The human skeleton called Kennewick Man found near the city of the same name in 1996 has been dated to about 9,000 years ago (see sidebar).

DON'T GET BITTEN BY A RATTLESNAKE

If it's summer, almost anywhere in the Channeled Scablands you might encounter a rattlesnake. Although absent for most of the fall and winter months, they thrive here in the spring and summer, soaking up the sun in the morning hours and retreating to shady niches in the heat of the day. Rattlers often blend in with the colors of basalt rock, so listen for the telltale rattling sound. Don't reach under rocks or logs. Wear boots and protect your lower legs when hiking scabland trails. They will likely hear you first and slither away long before you encounter them, but take precautions.

The earliest Native Americans likely lived a nomadic life in the Columbia Plateau region and traveled from one water source to another, gathering wild food that grew in the native soils. As we move much closer to the present day, we know that Native Americans lived all along the Columbia and Snake rivers, with tribes including the Spokane, Nespelem, and Okanogan living in the north scablands and the Yakama, Walla Walla, Umatilla, and other tribes living in the southern region. The first few peaceful encounters between these peoples and white explorers took place when Lewis and Clark and, later, Canadian explorer David Thompson passed through here in the early years of the nineteenth century.

AGRICULTURE IN THE SCABLANDS

In the ensuing decades, more easterners moved west, some to become involved in various gold rushes, others heading west to start ranches and farms. Although the scabland channels quickly received a deserved reputation as earth that was unyielding to the plow, surrounding regions such as the Palouse Hills east of the scablands and other terrain north of the Telford–Crab Creek scabland area were regions of rich soil where a variety of crops could be grown.

Other farmers saw their agricultural ventures fail, however, when they tried to grow crops in places where the floods had passed through thousands

KENNEWICK MAN

On July 28, 1996, the skeletal remains of a prehistoric man were discovered on a bank of the Columbia River in Kennewick. The accidental find was made by two spectators attending the annual hydroplane races held nearby. Their discovery turned out to be one of the most complete ancient skeletons ever found. Tests have dated the skeleton between 5,650 and 9,510 years old. Most peoples' familiarity with Kennewick Man was the result of news coverage about the nine-year legal proceedings between scientists, the federal government, and Native American tribes who claimed Kennewick Man as their ancestor. A 2004 court ruling allowed scientific research on the skeleton to continue.

Relic from Folsom Farms, near Fishtrap Lake

of years earlier. In his many years of wandering through the scablands from the 1920s on, J Harlen Bretz noted the many hopeful farmers he met who had tried to farm hills they thought were rich with Palouse soil but were actually huge gravel bars left from the ice-age floods, topped with only a thin layer of earth. Perhaps an even more significant factor in the demise of many farms and ranches in the early twentieth century were the droughts and dust storms of the 1920s, followed by the Great Depression of the 1930s.

To improve the capabilities of farmers and ranchers on the Columbia Plateau, as well as to stimulate a stagnant economy, the Franklin Roosevelt administration and its "New Deal" operations determined that a source for irrigation water in the dry Columbia Plateau region was the answer to the problems of area farmers. Building Grand Coulee Dam promised a wide distribution of water throughout the scablands region through a complex system of canals. But World War II saw a switch in priorities. With the dam now assigned to power production, the facility's irrigation component would have to wait until victory overseas was realized.

The grid of canals was finally completed in the 1950s, converting thousands of acres from sagebrush to fields of wheat, potatoes, and other crops, particularly between Interstate 90 and US Highway 2 from Spokane west to the Big Bend of the Columbia River. While these areas were rich with crops because of the water the farmers could now bring to their land, the basalt-strewn scabland channels and flood-scoured flatlands remained resistant to farming.

From the time of the earliest human existence to the large farming and ranching operations found in the region today, human history in the Channeled Scablands has been one of humans pitted against the natural elements and succeeding to a degree in taming the land around them. But the scablands have also succeeded: their sheer rawness and inability to be irrigated, planted, and tamed drove many settlers away in defeat, while convincing others to leave certain parts of the land as they had first found it—ragged, rough, and windblown.

Opposite page: *Hiker on trail to Towell Falls, Escure Ranch*

THREE

GETTING AROUND IN THE CHANNELED SCABLANDS

In Washington, the Channeled Scablands are bounded on the north roughly by US Highway 2, from Spokane west to nearly Coulee City, where the boundary heads due north to the Columbia River at Coulee Dam; from there the Columbia forms the rest of the northern boundary, as well as the western boundary south to near Mattawa. From Mattawa, the boundary continues due south to the Oregon border. The eastern boundary of the scablands is a little west of US 195, from Spokane south to the Snake River, which forms the southern boundary west to the Tri Cities, where the boundary again follows the Columbia. The Columbia and Snake River watersheds contain most of the scabland area.

This chapter provides an overview of the entire region, from getting around in the scablands, whether driving, hiking, or paddling, as well as a section on how information is organized in this guide. The gateway communities are Wenatchee and Vantage in the west, the Tri Cities in the south, and Spokane in the northeast corner. The primary east-west routes within the Channeled Scablands are US 2 in the north, Interstate 90 in the middle, and State Route 26 in the south. Major north-south routes include US 195 just east of the scablands, US 395 angling southwest from Spokane, and US 97 heading north from US 2 to follow the Columbia to Brewster (and beyond). Connecting these primary highways are many smaller state highways, which are described within each chapter in Part II.

THE FIVE MAJOR SCABLAND REGIONS

In this book, I have divided the scabland tracts in Washington into five regions primarily defined by their geographic locations, though these divisions also reflect differences in climate, vegetation, and the types of scabland features. These five regions, traveling from northeast to southwest just like the ice-age floods, are the Cheney-Palouse Scabland, the Telford–Crab Creek Tract, Grand and Moses Coulees, Moses Lake–Quincy Basin, and the Pasco–Lake Lewis Basins.

Part II of this guide covers each of these five regions in depth, describing the overall environment of each area, the scabland features to be found there, activities to be enjoyed (such as hiking, bicycling, and paddling), and some ideas for driving routes you might take, including time guidelines—how

Road along floor below Dry Falls

many hours you should plan to spend visiting an area and exploring the various geologic and other attractions in the scablands.

DRIVING THE SCABLANDS

To make any headway, visitors to the scablands pretty much have to explore by car, since the area is so huge and the features so widely dispersed. Some of the features are easy to see from the road or on a short jaunt from a parking area, but many require a little more effort—extensive driving on unpaved roads and/or a hike, whether short or a bit longer. When driving in the scablands, make sure your car is in good running condition and equipped with emergency supplies, because it can be a long ways between towns with services. If you plan on driving unpaved roads, make sure you have good tires and clearance. And whether you explore via auto, on foot, or in a boat, make sure you have a good map and know how to use it. See the section on the Washington Department of Fish and Wildlife near the end of this chapter regarding Discover Pass requirements for some areas in the scablands.

HIKING AND BICYCLING THE SCABLANDS

If you plan on taking walks or bike rides in the scablands, equip yourself as you would for any backcountry excursion, including the ten essentials.

Gear for sun protection is mandatory: sunscreen, sunglasses, a wide-brimmed hat, long-sleeved shirt and pants, and plenty of water. No matter what time of year you hike or bike in the scablands, you'll probably be exposed to lots of sun—as well as wind and maybe the occasional rain shower. Be prepared for cold or wet weather according to the season you plan to travel. Remember, it gets very cold in winter, so short outings may be all you can endure at that time of year. See the section on the Bureau of Land Management (BLM) near the end of this chapter regarding regulations on BLM land.

THE TEN ESSENTIALS

1. Navigation (map and compass)
2. Sun protection (sunglasses and sunscreen)
3. Insulation (extra clothing)
4. Illumination (headlamp or flashlight)
5. First-aid supplies
6. Fire (firestarter and matches/lighter)
7. Repair kit and tools (including knife)
8. Nutrition (extra food)
9. Hydration (extra water)
10. Emergency shelter

—The Mountaineers

EXPLORING THE SCABLANDS ON HORSEBACK

The same advice as above applies to those who venture into the scablands on horseback—and you will also need to take into consideration your mount's needs for water. A number of destinations in the scablands are particularly well suited for horses. Some even have corrals where you can place your horse while camping close by. Lands managed by the BLM are especially receptive to use by equestrians. Among the best places to ride are Escure Ranch, in the Cheney-Palouse Scabland, and Lakeview Ranch, in the Telford–Crab Creek Tract.

EXPLORING THE SCABLANDS BY WATER

This book deals largely with scenic and geologically significant locales within the Channeled Scablands that can be toured by car, on foot, by bicycle, and on horseback, but in many places you can see scabland scenery from a boat as well. In most cases, you will find that your perspective changes dramatically when you are viewing geologic features from the water rather than a highway or trail. So if you have a canoe, a kayak, or even a fishing boat, you can use your watercraft in a great number of places within the Channeled Scablands. The examples outlined briefly below provide ideas of scenic spots you can explore by water; more detailed descriptions can be found throughout Part II. A great guide to canoe and kayak opportunities in the scablands is *Paddle Routes of the Inland Northwest* by Rich Landers and Dan Hansen (see Recommended Resources at the back of this book).

As with any outing on a lake or river, observe the usual safety precautions and bring along sunscreen, a hat, food, water, a map, and a life jacket. A camera is another handy thing to bring.

Cheney-Palouse Scabland

Nearly all of the *kolk* lakes found in the Cheney-Palouse Scabland that are not on private land are accessible by small fishing boats, canoes, or kayaks. Medical, Silver, Williams, and Badger lakes are the most likely to be congested in summer months, when you'll need to be aware of power boats,

Boat dock on north end of Fishtrap Lake

BRETZ'S CLUES

J Harlen Bretz once wrote that the topography of the Channeled Scablands was "river-bottom topography magnified to the proportion of river-valley topography." And this was key to the lack of understanding by so many of his contemporaries in the geological profession. They were so attuned to the normal processes of river valley creation that it defied logic and convention to imagine any other cause to explain the formation of this region. When Bretz was able to divorce himself from this standard methodology, then he was able to imagine other possible modes of creation, and the true causes of the features in the landscape before him revealed themselves.

water skiers, and tubers that might be sharing the same waterways with you. If you're looking for a quiet paddle on these and other lakes close to the Spokane urban area, the early morning hours are best and weekdays are better than weekends, for obvious reasons.

Telford–Crab Creek Tract

Many of the lakes in the Telford–Crab Creek Tract are small *kolk* lakes that can be seen in their entirety from the shore. They might be more truthfully called ponds, in some instances. Others are on private land and virtually inaccessible for exploration. A handful of lakes in this area do offer some paddling and boating opportunities, however (see Part II).

Grand and Moses Coulees

Lakes enclosed by the walls of the Grand and Moses coulees tend to be either really big (like Banks Lake) or really small (like Jameson Lake). The really big ones mean more competition with power boats, personal watercraft, and anglers. The really small ones mean few services and limited lake surface to paddle around on. Both types of lakes, however, offer the spectacular environment found only in coulee lakes—that otherworldly sense of being in some hidden world enclosed by towering rock walls and isolated from the rest of the world.

Fishing is popular at Deep Lake.

Large lakes offer developed facilities where you can put in. Smaller lakes offer a single boat launch, often a place where the grass or earthen shoreline simply happens to slope down to the water. Either way, you haven't experienced that feeling of solitude, adventure, and mystery that comes with exploring a sunken, basalt-lined, and hidden world if you haven't launched your fishing boat, canoe, rowboat, or kayak in the waters of a coulee lake.

Moses Lake–Quincy Basin

Paddling and rowing opportunities are many and varied in the Moses Lake–Quincy Basin area. Aside from the two giants here—Moses Lake and Potholes Reservoir—some of the best lakes are found within the wild, eroded environs of the Drumheller Channels (see Part II).

Pasco–Lake Lewis Basins

Most boating opportunities in this region of the scablands are found in the waters of the Columbia and Snake rivers.

A ROAD BY ANY OTHER NAME

When you travel back roads, you gaze at a lot of maps and learn the names of a lot of roads. Sometimes you can't help making some interesting observations. The first thing I noticed when I started cataloging the names of scabland roads was that they tend to fall into six basic categories. The following groupings of road names seem to account for just about every dirt,

Highway 23 passes through scabland terrain east of Sprague.

gravel, and blacktop thoroughfare found on the floor of every coulee and atop every craggy basalt plateau in the scablands.

PEOPLES' NAMES

Having a road named for you is apparently quite an honor. Roads that are named after someone seem to imply that the person so honored is quite important by having his name on a road sign. And, should you wonder, I use the word "his" on purpose. There are scores of roads in the Channeled Scablands named after men, but very few are named after women.

Examples include *George Knott Road*, *Charles Jordan Road*, *Gene Nelson Road*, and *Herman Road*. I'm assuming that most of these roads lead to the homes of the men whose names are on the road signs. Or cross their land. Or perhaps the individual whose name is on the road sign is a local leader or elected official or was responsible for the road in question being built in the first place.

In any case, it seems odd that there are few if any roads in the scablands named after women. In fact, it occurs to me that some of those ranchers out there in the scablands might be smart to name their roads after their wives or lady friends. What a gift to give your wife or sweetheart on Valentines Day—name a road after her! When a road is named after you, you can actually go to see your road, even drive up and down it all day if you like.

FUNCTIONAL NAMES

These are roads very logically named after the business or enterprise found at the end of the road. Examples include *Game Farm Road, Fish Hatchery Road,* and *Seven Springs Dairy Road.* These are honest, straightforward monikers for roads. If you pull onto *Fish Hatchery Road*, by golly, you're going to end up at a fish hatchery!

GEOLOGIC NAMES

Many roads in the scablands are named for the natural geologic features they pass through or take you to. If you're not sure how to get to Dry Coulee, for example, taking *Dry Coulee Road* is probably a safe decision. More examples include *Rock Lake Road, Baird Springs Road, Jameson Lake Road,* and *Lance Hill Road.*

ROADS BETWEEN TOWNS

Some scabland towns are separated from the next by miles and miles of dry flood channels and desolate stretches of sage-covered terrain, so it probably made sense to string roads between them and name the road for both towns, thereby letting people know what's at both ends of the highway. Examples include *Cheney-Spangle Road*, *Pasco-Kahlotus Road*, *Ralston-Benge Road*, and *Waverly-Plaza Road*. The only conceivable problem might be if you arrived at one of these roads via some rutted and mud-encrusted earthen track that suddenly dropped you off on a paved highway with the names of two towns on it. The dilemma? Which town lies in which direction?

BEAN COUNTER ROADS

I find it surprising and a bit distressing that large sections of the scablands—particularly in Grant and Adams Counties—have roads with functional but incredibly boring names that offer only directional data. Examples include *Road 4 SW, Road H NW,* and *Road Q SE.* I often wonder what wistful, creative, and intriguing bean counter in the back room of some county office came up with such romantic and colorful appellations.

HISTORICAL NAMES

I love being exposed to history whenever I explore the scablands, so I really enjoy taking roads that reflect times gone by—or maybe "roads gone by" is more accurate. Who but some avid historian could come up with names like *Old SR 26 Road, Old Highway Loop,* and *Old Moses Lake Highway* (is it an old highway or an old lake?). Then there's my favorite: *Old Missile Silo Road.* So does that mean there's a new missile silo somewhere in the same vicinity? I'd like to know, just to be on the safe side.

MY PERSONAL FAVORITES

Some roads just make you smile—for instance, *Detour Road* in northern Lincoln County. By its very nature, a detour is temporary, right? But this road has a permanent sign and has been called this for years. So what am I detouring *from* when I take *Detour Road?* And what would happen if *Detour Road* had to be temporarily closed for some reason? What would they name the road that provided a detour from *Detour Road?*

One of my favorite roads is *Beverly Burke Road,* in Adams County. I have no idea where that name came from, but it sounds to me like a fitting name for a female client of Perry Mason's.

Lincoln County's *Fink Road* always makes me chuckle. *Muse Road,* near Othello, makes me think I'm going to come upon some guy stopped in his car along the side of the road, simply musing the day away. *Wise Road,* near LaCrosse, sounds as though it was designed exclusively for the use of intellectual, discriminating drivers. I try to take this road every opportunity I get.

BUREAU OF LAND MANAGEMENT ACCESS

One interesting consequence of exploring a region connected by its geologic past but spread out over some 2,000 square miles is that you find yourself crossing parcels of land with a diverse collection of owners. Depending where you are in the scablands, the land might be owned by a city, a county, the state, an entity of the federal government, or a private landowner. Federal ownership of land comes in two chief guises: Bureau of Land Management

(BLM) lands and US Fish and Wildlife parcels. In both cases, the terrain is freely open to public exploration with only minimal regulations.

In some of our country's most wide-open western states—Nevada and Utah are good examples—the BLM oversees upward of 30 to 40 percent of the states' lands. In Washington State, that figure is less than 10 percent—but that's still thousands of square miles of terrain, and much of it is spectacular scabland topography, some parcels easily among the most scenic within the eastern Washington region.

As a teenager (long before arthritis began to take its toll on knees and ankles), I actively sought out BLM land in the Mojave Desert precisely because I knew that on BLM parcels, I could hike for hours across a variety of landscapes with few, if any, improvements and even fewer restrictions on my movement. As much as I enjoy visiting state parks and national parks, I am happiest when exploring public lands with few roads, fewer signs, and a bare minimum of rules and regulations. Not that I can't play nice and follow the rules of polite society, but there's just something about hiking across raw ground that feels so much better to me than moving along a marked trail or paved path or wooden boardwalk. In the scablands, there is also the lingering ghostly presence of J Harlen Bretz, who completed most of his scabland field outings by traveling cross-country on foot, without any semblance of the reliable regional maps we have at our disposal today.

Coral Lake in Drumheller Channels

Trailhead for the hiking path near Hog Lake

Most of the BLM lands found throughout the United States were initially put under the agency's control as a means to protect sensitive species or significant geologic features. The BLM's stated mission is "to sustain the health, diversity, and productivity of the public lands for the use and enjoyment of present and future generations." To uphold this mission, some minor restrictions are placed on visitors to BLM lands to protect one or more plant or animal species, cultural artifacts, or physical features of the land that deserve protection.

These restrictions, however, are minimal and not consistent from one BLM tract to another. In some cases, motorized vehicles are restricted to access roads and exploration must be on foot, horseback, or mountain bike. At other locations, hunting is prohibited. Open fires are sometimes banned due to fire danger, either seasonally or year-round. Other than these reasonable restrictions imposed when necessary, BLM land is pretty much open for exploration with few rules and regulations.

There is only one possible drawback to BLM land that I can come up with: the scattered and somewhat checkerboard layout of BLM parcels, which often is created by acquiring land in a somewhat piecemeal fashion from a variety of private owners. As a result, you might be hiking across BLM public land and suddenly cross an invisible line to find yourself on private ranch land. There are not always fences or signage to let you know this has happened, but each parcel of BLM land has a corresponding map that is clearly marked and available free from the BLM office in Spokane. More detailed topographic maps or GPS devices can also be helpful items to carry with you when visiting parcels of land that are overseen by the BLM.

The BLM also has available for a nominal fee an incredible map of Lincoln County showing scabland channels and flood areas as well as locations of all BLM parcels within the Lincoln County area. My copy became dog-eared with constant use after a few months and will no doubt need to be replaced on a regular basis, so much do I rely on it.

The BLM's Spokane office is located at 1103 North Fancher Road, Spokane, WA 99212; (509) 536-1200. The BLM's Wenatchee Office is located at 915 Walla Walla Avenue, Wenatchee WA 98801; (509) 665-2100.

WASHINGTON DEPARTMENT OF FISH AND WILDLIFE DISCOVER PASSES

Many locations in the Channeled Scablands, wild and desolate as they may seem, require a Washington Department of Fish and Wildlife (WDFW) permit, also known as a Discover Pass, which hangs from your vehicle's rear-view mirror. Sites requiring these permits are clearly identified with signage, but I recommend that you just break down and buy one, then put it on your vehicle's rear-view mirror ahead of any trip out into the scablands. Better safe than sorry, in other words.

A Discover Pass costs $35 and is available at any business in Washington selling fishing and hunting licenses. Passes can also be ordered online for $35. To check on the latest rules and fees, go to http://wdfw.wa.gov/licensing.

SOME WORDS OF CAUTION: IT'S EASY TO DIE OUT HERE

Let's talk danger for a moment. I suggest this topic only after a few brief moments of hesitation, since it has always been my contention that nature regularly presents us with life-or-death challenges as a means to thin out our population, and who am I to interfere with this natural process? Indeed, people who boldly stroll toward the lip of a 400-foot dry waterfall and cannot manage to stop in time to avoid plummeting over the edge should possibly consider limiting their experiences with nature to the type of adventures offered through the Discovery Channel. Nevertheless, with some misgivings, I offer these few warnings.

Don't be stupid in the park.

A sign to heed!

The Channeled Scablands region, by virtue of its wildness and relatively untamed and lightly visited terrain, is generally not fenced off or strewn with caution signs to safely guide you along your merry way. Indeed, the very dramatic and breathtaking views that await you around many corners are just the sort of vistas that are likely to draw you to your doom if you're not awake and aware of your surroundings.

That said, let's look at some of the clear and present dangers found in the scablands, in the hopes that you will avoid the most prevalent obstacles and pitfalls to be encountered if you spend any time at all in eastern Washington's Columbia Plateau territory.

Places You Can Fall

Let's start with places where you have a pretty decent chance of falling off a cliff if you're not careful. Williams Lake has a plunge pool with a 100-foot drop—and no warning sign. The Dry Falls and Palouse Falls overlooks, though they have warning signs and fences, are still places to watch your step. Potholes and Frenchman coulees and Wallula Gap have outstanding views, but stay away from the edge.

Places You Can Drown

Crab Creek, Canniwai Creek, Wilson Creek, Palouse River, Snake River, Columbia River, Banks Lake, Badger Lake, Williams Lake, Sprague Lake, Rock Lake, Hog Lake, Fishtrap Lake, Lenore Lake, Soap Lake, Billy Clapp Lake . . . well, you get the picture.

Places You Can Bash Your Head

Any place and any time you are hiking along the rough, uneven, scrabbly surfaces of scabland terrain you can slip and hurt yourself. In basalt caves and crevices with low ceilings you can easily bash your head. The same is true anyplace with overhanging ledges, falling rocks, basalt columns, and steep slopes of talus. So . . . wear a hat. Stand up slowly. Don't take shortcuts on switchbacks. Watch for falling rocks. And keep your head on your shoulders.

HOW TO USE THE REGIONAL TOUR GUIDE IN PART II

Each of the five major scabland regions has its own chapter, which begins with an overview of the major geologic features of the region. Next is a Towns section that describes the places where you might find services such as gas, food, lodging, supplies, and medical care. The Parks and Camping section lists the public facilities where you might find drinking water, restrooms, picnic tables, and campsites. Under each of the numbered scabland features you'll find a general description of that feature, followed by driving directions to it and information on activities such as hiking, bicycling, horseback riding, and boating. Each chapter concludes with a recommended auto tour or two.

Klink's Restaurant at Williams Lake

Throughout the book, sidebars add interesting notes and information along the way. At the back of the book you'll find a list of recommended reading and viewing for more information on the Channeled Scablands. As always, when traveling in remote regions, take precautions and check weather and road conditions before setting out on your adventure.

GUIDE TO THE ICONS

Hiking

Swimming

Canoeing and Kayaking

Fishing

Boating

Wildlife Viewing

Biking

Picnic Area

Mountain Biking

Camping

Horseback Riding

Auto Tour

Opposite page: *Coulee floor below Dry Falls is a moonscape of potholes and basalt boulders.*

PART II

Touring the Channeled Scablands

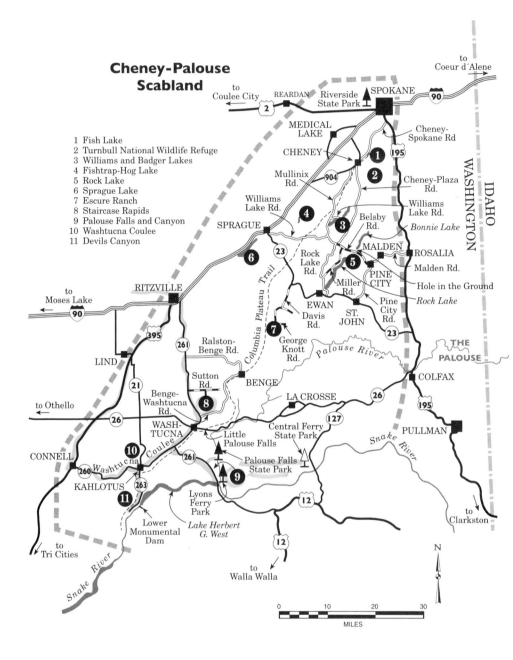

Cheney-Palouse Scabland

1 Fish Lake
2 Turnbull National Wildlife Refuge
3 Williams and Badger Lakes
4 Fishtrap-Hog Lake
5 Rock Lake
6 Sprague Lake
7 Escure Ranch
8 Staircase Rapids
9 Palouse Falls and Canyon
10 Washtucna Coulee
11 Devils Canyon

Opposite page: *A hiker on the converted old railroad grade above Rock Lake*

FOUR

CHENEY-PALOUSE SCABLAND

The Cheney-Palouse Scabland tract represents the easternmost path of the floodwaters that flowed across the Columbia Plateau dozens of times between 15,000 and 18,000 years ago. This tract of scabland ranges from 10 to 25 miles wide and is about 90 miles long. Covering about 1,500 square miles of scabland and nonscabland terrain, it is by far the largest of the three "tracts" of flood-carved channels. Like all scabland tracts, the elevation is highest in the north and drops as you travel south and west.

The region contains many lakes, all oriented in a northeast to southwest direction, and all carved out of basalt by the floodwaters. The largest and deepest of all scabland lakes, Rock Lake, is found here. A great deal of lore and legend—including a headless Native American chief and a sea serpent—revolves around this deep and shadowy gorge.

Largely due to the elevation and latitude of its most northerly sections, the Cheney-Palouse tract contains more forested land than other regions of the scablands. This means that scabland terrain such as potholes and unremitting ridges of basalt are sometimes cloaked in pines or adorned with ferns and small bushes, softening what would otherwise be very harsh-looking features if they were found in drier parts of the Columbia Plateau.

Among the many flood-carved attractions contained within this scabland tract is the curiosity of a river that was rerouted by the floodwaters. After winding its way westerly through miles of farmland and hill country, the Palouse River takes an abrupt turn south and passes through a deep canyon to join the Snake River, pausing long enough to drop 200 feet in an impressive waterfall.

Also found within this scabland tract are the remnants of a cascade of water now called Staircase Rapids. It is thought that floodwaters may have reached a speed of 70 miles per hour here. Not far to the southwest lies Devils Canyon, a dramatic flood-carved chasm that takes off at a right angle from Washtucna Coulee as it descends steeply toward the Snake River.

SCABLAND LAKES IN THIS REGION

Hundreds of potholes, ponds, and sizable lakes are found within the Cheney-Palouse Scabland tract. Nearly all of these lakes are surrounded by basalt

BRETZ'S CLUES

J Harlen Bretz's exploration of the Palouse Hills, Palouse Falls, and Washtucna Coulee were instrumental in this development of his radical theory about the formation of the Channeled Scablands: "Examination of altitudes," wrote Bretz, "shows that lower Crab Creek Valley and Washtucna Coulee must have contained backwater from the Gateway [Wallula Gap] and that this was very probably responsible for the high water levels which initiated Othello Channels and Devils Canyon divide crossings, and probably was a factor favoring the Drumheller Channels and Palouse Canyon crossings." Visiting these spots today, does your imagination stretch as big as Bretz's?

cliffs. Most are found just south of Spokane. The majority of lakes in this region are small and on private land. Some are situated alongside public roads, affording a glimpse from your car. To visit some of the larger, publicly accessible lakes, travel southwest from Spokane on I-90 and SR 904 through Cheney. (See the Cheney-Palouse Auto Tours at the end of this chapter.)

Nearly all lakes within the northern Cheney-Palouse Scabland tract are developed at least partially because of their proximity to urban areas. Some of the lakes not far from the Spokane metropolitan area include Medical Lake, Badger Lake, Williams Lake, Fish Lake, and Sprague Lake. On the shores of some lakes are campsites, trailer spaces, docks, and boat launches; others are the sites of restaurants and small general stores.

A distinctly less wild and more suburban atmosphere is found at more than a half dozen lakes surrounding the town of Medical Lake, including its namesake, where bathers sought improved health through medicinal minerals at the turn of the century. Other lakes here have names like Silver, Clear, Granite, and Willow. Homes line their shores, and boats are out on the water every summer for both fishing and water sports.

In and around the Turnbull National Wildlife Refuge, just south of Cheney, are dozens of smaller scabland lakes. They serve as habitat for more than 200 different types of birds that populate the area year-round and are a popular destination for birders. Not to be outdone by these avian visitors are a diverse collection of mammals including badgers, beavers, coyote, deer, elk, and porcupine.

Badger and Williams lakes are a bit farther south but still are the site of summer cabins, boat docks, small stores, and cafés. Though close to the Spokane-Cheney urban area, these and similar retreats offer a feeling of isolation because of the way they are situated down inside their deep, cliff-flanked flood channels.

While the private ownership of waterfront property means that some scabland lakes have been well-populated with *Homo sapiens*, other lakes have been saved from this fate for precisely the same reason. Because farmers and ranchers own the property surrounding scenic Rock Lake, Hole in the Ground, and Bonnie Lake, for example, no development has occurred here, and the landscape looks pretty much the same as it did when J Harlen Bretz trekked across it in the 1920s. Eight-mile-long Rock Lake is separated from smaller Bonnie Lake by a 3-mile strip of marshy bottomland, the Hole in the Ground, which is flanked by high basalt cliffs.

The only way to reach Bonnie Lake if you don't know the landowners is to take a kayak up Rock Creek (the land is private, but waterways are not) from the bridge that crosses the middle of Hole in the Ground. Massive Rock Lake, too, is hard to see unless you use private roads or hike along a state-owned right-of-way following the onetime route of a regional railroad line.

About 15 miles west of Rock Lake is the second-largest scabland lake, Sprague Lake, between 5 and 6 miles long. A vast no-man's land of dry gullies, eroded buttes, and standing pillars of columnar basalt separate the two bodies of water.

Circle tours are the best way to see two or more scabland lakes in one short drive from Spokane or Cheney, providing you with a good picture of what these bodies of water look like, the sort of terrain they are found in, and why they first struck geologist J Harlen Bretz as somewhat unusual way back in the 1920s.

TOWNS IN THE CHENEY-PALOUSE SCABLAND

- BENGE (pronounced like the second syllable in re-VENGE) is a small Adams County town northeast of Washtucna. It was named after Frank H. Benge, who represented the county in the State Legislature in 1904. Remains of a few old buildings make Benge a popular destination for ghost-town enthusiasts, though the town is very much alive. Some abandoned houses have been torn down in the past few years, but a wood-frame store and the desolate surroundings make Benge a unique and out-of-the-way spot to visit. There are virtually no services for nonresidents here, but there is one general store where snacks can be purchased.

- CHENEY is a thriving community with a population of nearly 11,000 about 17 miles southwest of Spokane on SR 904. Cheney is the home of Eastern Washington University and its 2011 championship football team! The town is also in a major farming and ranching area, which makes for an eclectic mix of rural landowners and professorial types gathering at local restaurants, coffee houses, stores, and events. All services can be found here, including medical care.

- KAHLOTUS, located smack dab in the middle of Washtucna Coulee, is at the junction of SR 260 and SR 263. A former railroad town dating from the 1880s, it now has just over 200 residents. In its prime, when railroad lines were being built all over eastern Washington, Kahlotus boasted nearly twenty saloons, a bank, a newspaper, brothels, and other businesses. Now, it's the gateway to Devils Canyon. Services consist of one small general store.

- LA CROSSE, in southwest Whitman County on SR 26, began its life as a town when two railroads created a junction here in 1888. The town was incorporated in 1917. Numbering just 400, La Crosse citizens are chiefly involved in agriculture. Services include a restaurant, a gas station, and two grocery stores.

- RITZVILLE, just north of I-90 at its junction with US 395 and SR 261, is a hub for surrounding farms. Services include gas, food, lodging, and a city park.

- SPOKANE, with a population of around 200,000, is the urban center of the Inland Empire; it has several colleges, and freight and passenger trains pass through daily. I-90, US 2, US 195, and US 395 all converge in Spokane. It has all services, including several hospitals, banks, and city parks.

- SPRAGUE is a historic community of about 500 in the scablands south of I-90, some 25 miles southwest of Spokane. Due to its location along a major transcontinental railroad, thousands of settlers and Scandinavian immigrants passed through the town and settled there on their way to Seattle back in the 1800s, when it was incorporated. There are gas stations, a restaurant or two, and even a hotel here. Sprague Lake is just south of town.

- ST. JOHN, located on SR 23 about 27 miles east of Sprague, was founded and named in the late 1880s for settler E. T. St. John. With just over 500 people, St. John is a pleasant little farming community in a rich agricultural area just east of a major scabland channel and mysterious Rock Lake, largest and deepest of the scabland lakes. Services include gas stations, groceries, and a bed-and-breakfast.

- WASHTUCNA, located at the head of the coulee bearing the same name, is at the junction of SR 26 and SR 261. It is considered the gateway to Palouse Falls. Washtucna has about 250 people, most of whom are involved in farming on the higher hills above the coulee. Crops grown include wheat, barley, canola, and alfalfa. Services include a bank, gas station, and tavern-restaurant.

PARKS AND CAMPING IN THE CHENEY-PALOUSE SCABLAND

- CENTRAL FERRY STATE PARK, on SR 127 south of LaCrosse, has picnic, camping, and swimming facilities and a boat launch on the Snake River.

- LYONS FERRY STATE PARK, on SR 261 at the Snake River, has camping, swimming, boating, and fishing.

- PALOUSE FALLS STATE PARK, east of SR 261, has picnic and camping facilities.

- RIVERSIDE STATE PARK, north of downtown Spokane, has picnic and camping facilities as well as trails both paved and unpaved. Fishing and horseback riding are popular here.

- WILLIAMS LAKE RESORT, on Williams Lake Road south of Cheney, has camping with hookups, a store, a rec room, a sports field, swimming, and a boat launch.

1 FISH LAKE

GETTING THERE: From Spokane, take US 195 south to Cheney-Spokane Road. Turn right and drive about 8.5 miles to the park entrance signs. At Myers Road, turn left and follow signs to the parking area.

Fish Lake was converted to a Spokane County Park nearly a decade ago and has expanded from a simple fishing lake to a neat little recreation lake for the whole family, just a few minutes' drive from Cheney. The 52-acre park offers a swimming beach, play equipment, hiking trails, even a basketball court. There are also picnic tables and barbecues. Only nonmotorized boats are allowed on this lake, where anglers fish for brook, brown, and tiger trout. It's also a great lake to paddle around in a canoe.

Winter at Fish Lake

2 TURNBULL NATIONAL WILDLIFE REFUGE

GETTING THERE: From SR 904 in Cheney, drive 4 miles south on the Cheney-Plaza Road. The refuge entrance is marked by a large entrance sign and arrow pointing down Smith Road. Drive about 2 miles east on Smith Road to reach the refuge headquarters and public-use area. The environmental education classroom is located at the refuge headquarters. **REGULATIONS:** Open during daylight hours only; nominal daily fee required March 1 to October 31

One of the best pieces of federally owned and managed scabland landscapes is the Turnbull National Wildlife Refuge, just 6 miles east from Cheney and 20 miles southwest of Spokane. The 16,000 acres that make up the refuge are composed of wetlands, lakes, basalt outcroppings, grassland, and forest—chiefly ponderosa pines and aspen groves.

Of the thousands of visitors to the 2,300-acre section accessible by the public, most come to see the birds and mammals that populate the region year-round, but especially during migratory seasons. Birds in particular are what draw the largest number of visitors to Turnbull. Commonly seen here are ducks, geese, swans, pelicans, and other water birds. Migrant songbirds and cavity-nesting birds such as nuthatches, chickadees, and woodpeckers can be watched from several locations within the preserve.

Mammals wandering about the refuge range from tiny chipmunks to deer, elk, moose, and cougar. As with most wildlife preserves, it can be tricky to catch a glimpse of animal residents unless you are very patient, and sometimes they can only be viewed early in the morning.

A 5.5-mile paved loop road can be driven, ridden on bikes, or hiked to get a good feel for the terrain and its inhabitants. The loop road includes a chance to enjoy an overlook trail (Kepple Lake), two accessible trails (Kepple Lake Interpretive Trail and Pine Lake Loop Trail), and a walk at Black Horse Lake (Boardwalk Trail). At certain times of the year, a user's fee may apply.

Boardwalk Trail at Black Horse Lake

3 WILLIAMS AND BADGER LAKES

GETTING THERE: From Cheney, head south on Main Street (SR 904) to the junction with Cheney-Plaza Road. Go south on this road for about 12 miles and make a right onto Williams Lake Road. To get to Badger Lake, stay on Williams Lake Road for about 2.5 miles, then turn right on Badger Lake Road; travel about 1.5 miles to Badger Lake. At the junction of Williams Lake Road and Badger Lake Road are the

Williams Lake is 3 miles long and flanked—as are most scabland lakes—with high basalt cliffs. Badger Lake is a little over 2 miles long and a bit narrower than Williams Lake, with more coves and bends in the shore; high basalt cliffs line both sides of this water-filled trough. As floodwaters carved out these lakes, the falls separating them receded to the point we see today. Both lakes are located about 15 miles south of Cheney.

The dry falls and plunge pool below are worth seeing, but be careful at the steep, unprotected edge of the drop-off. There are dry falls separating the two lake basins. To get to Williams Lake, continue down Williams Lake Road less than 1 mile to a turnout for the Williams Lake Resort on your left.

no warning signs of any kind here, although you'd have to keep your eyes closed to miss the approach to the 100-foot drop as you move toward it. I suppose you could get your feet wet by stepping into (rather than jumping across) one of the miniature streams that run across the upper ledge of the dry cascade's rocky lip. And slippery feet are not recommended while strolling up to the edge of a precipice. Then there's the possibility of being so enthralled with the view that you don't realize you are at the edge of the semicircular dry waterfall before it's too late. Suffice to say, be careful here and always aware of your surroundings. If you have small children with you, please take them by the hand. Dogs should be on a leash as well, because the edge of the drop-off appears rather suddenly, and it is about 100 feet down to the pile of sharp-edged basalt talus below. So few people stop to check this place out that you may be waiting awhile for any help.

Williams Lake is a popular getaway for Spokane-area residents. The lake is stocked with rainbow and cutthroat trout, and fishing can be rewarding. The lake is also great for water-skiing and tubing, as locals and Spokane-area visitors will attest. The unofficial "season" at Williams is April through September; not all businesses and activities on the lake are available during other months.

There are two resorts on the lake, but keep in mind that the loosely employed word "resort" in this neck of the woods can mean a general store,

Dry cataract between Williams and Badger lakes

café, and trailer spaces. In the case of Williams Lake, there are two resorts, one on each end of the lake. Family-owned and -operated Bunker's Resort offers cabin rental, RV parking, and camping spaces. A western-themed bar and grill serves breakfast, lunch, and dinner at reasonable prices. The resort offers a public boat launch, swimming, and fishing.

Williams Lake Resort is a seasonal RV resort open April through September. Sixty full and partial RV hookups, tent sites, and rental cabins are offered. Fishing boats with motors can be rented, as well as kayaks and paddleboats for the kids. The swimming area boasts a sandy beach and a swim platform with slide. More than seventy seasonal and permanent residents live here, giving this resort the feel of a small town, complete with general store. What sets the resort apart is Klink's, a gourmet restaurant (reservations required: 509-235-2391) located here among the pines and willows of this quaint lakeside community.

Badger Lake has one small area of trailers, a boat launch, and homes surrounding parts of the lake, but it doesn't have quite the level of activity found at Williams Lake.

4 FISHTRAP–HOG LAKE RECREATION AREA

GETTING THERE: Take I-90 to about 25 miles south of Spokane and take exit 254, then follow signs to Fishtrap Lake, about 3 miles. A map of the BLM-managed recreation area is available at the BLM offices in Spokane (see chapter 3). Maps are also available at the Ranch House Information Center in

I've always been fascinated with natural places that make you feel as though you're out in the middle of nowhere when you're actually just a short drive from a major urban area. The Fishtrap–Hog Lake Recreation Area is one of these magical places, and Hog Lake is one of the most peaceful lakes to visit. Just off I-90 about 25 miles southwest of Spokane, this is a rugged area of pine trees and scabland lakes the Fishtrap BLM area. More information can also be found in *Paddle Routes of the Inland Northwest* (see Recommended Resources). **REGULATIONS:** Wildlife area restrictions, posted fishing season, occasional road closures

and marshes, abandoned farm buildings, and breathtaking stair-step waterfalls.

A piece of regional history is found here at Folsom Farms, where the remains of early 1900s farm buildings recall a time when early settlers tried to make a go of farming and ranching. The silence of these buildings is in perfect synch with the natural solitude of the forested hills, soggy marshes, and rocky outcroppings that surround these remnants of a time long gone.

The major feature of this area—at least in terms of size—is Fishtrap Lake, a 3-mile-long, flood-created *kolk* lake flanked by high basalt cliffs; it is so narrow in spots that you might think you're navigating a river, not a lake. Less than a mile north is picturesque Hog Lake, a much smaller body of water. At the northern end of Hog Lake, accessible by boat or hiking trails, are two multitiered or stair-step-style waterfalls in a narrow area near the lake. These falls can be reached from a few faint footpaths that follow the floors of the canyons through which the streams and waterfalls flow.

At this BLM-managed recreation area, 14 miles of trails wind around the two lakes, trail through wet meadowlands, and pass within view of basalt outcrops and scabland trenches. Typical of the northern scablands, the rolling hills here are covered by pine forests and filled with native eastern Washington vegetation such as camas, serviceberry, lupine, and balsamroot.

Scenic Hog Lake

Watchable wildlife locations within the recreation area offer the chance to view American kestrels, prairie falcons, red-tailed hawks, and red-breasted nuthatches, to name just a few. As you hike along the edge of marshes or near the shores of the two major lakes here, you may spot a tiger salamander, spotted frog, or spadefoot toad. If you're hiking the trails during summer months, keep a lookout for rattlesnakes.

Local anglers fish for trout at Fishtrap and Hog lakes. At the north end of popular Fishtrap Lake you'll find a lakeside community, docks, and a café; boats with motors are allowed, but no water-skiing is permitted. For this reason, you're not likely to run into fast-moving boat traffic. The unique aspect of the smaller Hog Lake, as you'll note on the sign near its boat launch, is that fishing season is December through March. No, that sign is not a mistake—only ice fishing is allowed at Hog Lake, though summertime boating (powerboats not allowed) and canoeing are more than encouraged.

5 ROCK LAKE AND ENVIRONS

GETTING THERE: A visit to Rock Lake is a somewhat roundabout exercise in patience and possible frustration, although the south end of the lake can be reached easily enough: from Sprague take SR 23 about 14 miles east to the nearly nonexistent town of Ewan, then take Rock Lake Road north about 2 miles to the south end of the lake. The cliffs are lower here, without the dramatic gorge effect at the north end.

If they ever held a competition for "most mysterious lake" in Washington State, Rock Lake would have my vote. "That place is just creepy" is how my twenty-three-year-old son puts it. And nothing scares him.

Rock Lake is the longest and deepest of the scabland lakes; 300-foot basalt cliffs tower above the 8-mile-long lake and extend straight down to the water, then descend for another 400 feet below its surface.

Just about every facet of Rock Lake is entwined with mystery. Even its geologic past is intriguing. The lake lies in one of three deep depressions running from northeast to southwest and linked by Rock Creek. The three massive divots were created by intense glacial flooding. The other two are Hole in the Ground, a deep gash in the ground with fertile soil that now serves as pastureland, and Bonnie Lake, a smaller version of Rock Lake farther north.

Some geologists think that the formation of these three areas was linked to a fourth—Chapman Lake, which is northwest of the others and connected to them by a canyon tracking from the northwest to southeast. This runs counter to the normal northeast-to-southwest pattern of flood channels in the scablands, but it's likely that a natural fault line existing before the glacial flooding determined the path that floodwaters would take.

Rock Lake, Hole in the Ground, and Bonnie Lake are extreme examples of inaccessibility due to private land ownership. Rock Lake's only public access and boat launch are at its southern end. The only road to Hole in the Ground bisects its length, and the land on either side of the road is private. Bonnie Lake is completely surrounded by private land, and few people ever see it. One fortunate thing is that laws governing public access to bodies of water in Washington allow those with kayaks or canoes to visit these places, but doing so means paddling up Rock Creek for about a mile.

Rock Lake's water is incredibly cold, and this is not a good swimming lake. Winds are regularly channeled down the gorge that holds the lake, creating giant waves that have capsized boats. The sheer cliffs and lack of any shoreline or beaches to head for in emergencies add to the elements that make this a very unfriendly boating lake. Also contributing to the danger

A view of the north end of Rock Lake

are spears of sharp-edged basalt that lie just below the surface of the lake in some spots. These can rip into the hull of your boat if you're not careful to steer clear of these obstacles.

Rock Lake has always been shrouded by an element of intrigue. For centuries, Native Americans in the region have told stories of a sea serpent in the lake that would rip the bottoms out of Native American canoes and swallow the occupants. To this day, strange currents on the surface of the lake—likely caused by the wind funneled through the deep channel—only serve to sustain the legend. Some believe there may be one or more huge sturgeon in the deep lake, a theory that is nearly as compelling as that of a sea serpent. If there really are giant sturgeon here, could they be the ancestors of fish that washed in during the glacial floods thousands of years ago?

Another legend about the lake involves the rail line that ran atop the rocky cliffs on the east side of the lake. Sometime in the early 1900s, it is said that several cars of a train derailed and plummeted into a deep section of the lake. The cars were filled with brand-new Model T cars. The murkiness of Rock Lake's water, combined with its depth and no clues as to a precise location, means divers have come up empty so far. But it's one more great legend revolving around the lake. The rails of the former Chicago, Milwaukee, and St. Paul Railway have been removed, and the abandoned bed is now mostly state owned and accessible as a hiking-biking trail with advance reservations and a permit obtained from the Columbia Plateau Trail Central office in Washtucna (509-646-9218 or CPT.Central@Parks.wa.gov).

Other historical footnotes have only increased the intriguing, yet somewhat foreboding, atmosphere exuded by Rock Lake and its environs. Moonshiners worked in this area during prohibition, and an old cave with abandoned liquor processing equipment is said to exist in the basalt cliffs above the west side of the lake. A turn-of-the-twentieth-century resort hotel at the southern end of the lake can be seen in old photos but has been reduced to merely a few foundations now. Hotel guests used to descend to the lake by a steep staircase that led to a dock where they would board a covered excursion boat that offered tours of the lake, accompanied by phonograph records providing background theme music.

Perhaps the most famous, and regrettable, historical fact involves Native American Chief Kamiakin, who lived on land near the south end of the lake.

Kamiakin died in 1877 and was buried near the lake, but a visiting archae-ologist in 1878 found out about the chief's burial, located the grave, dug up the body, and removed the head for some bizarre reason. The chief was reburied by grieving relatives, but the missing head was never recovered.

Though geologic oddities abound around Rock Lake, most are on private land, and permission must be obtained to see them. A rare natural bridge of basalt can be found at the north end of Hole in the Ground. Near the road through this canyon is the Devils Well, a natural volcanic hole in the rock that was said to descend 100 feet or more before locals partially filled it with rocks to make it safer. Several natural caves in the basalt cliffs above the lake can be seen, and south of Rock Lake, "blow holes" can be found in the basalt. These are tunnels that pass all the way through the base of basalt cliffs and were likely caused by bubbles of air and steam that were active while the basalt was still hot and the cliffs were forming.

Although a look at Rock Lake might seem to consist of disjointed snapshots from various angles and not the sort of complete picture you get when visiting other bodies of water, it's still worth your time to take a look at the biggest, deepest, and—in my mind—eeriest of all scabland lakes.

The closest thing to a drive around the lake is to continue north on Rock Lake Road for about 2 miles, then take a right on Miller Road, which rises above the lake and offers fleeting views from its west shoreline. This is a dirt and gravel road; depending on the time of year, it is sometimes riddled with ruts and erosion-caused channels that can grab your tires and pull you this way and that.

To get a good view of the Hole in the Ground area, continue along Miller Road, then turn right on Belsby Road at the north end of Miller Road. You also can approach Belsby Road by driving south from Cheney on Cheney-Plaza Road, which turns into Rock Lake Road and meets up with Belsby Road after about 17 miles. Whichever way you reach Belsby Road, follow it east about 3 miles and descend into Hole in the Ground. At the bridge in the middle of the canyon, you can get out of your car and take photos of the area. Looking back to where you descended into Hole in the Ground, you can see the Devils Well to the left of the road you came down. Remember that the land on both sides of the road is private. To make a loop, ascend the east side of the Hole in the Ground by following Hole in the Ground Road to Stephen Road, then turn on

Pine City–Malden Road—either left (north) through the small towns of Pine City and Malden to Rosalia on US 195, or right (south) to St. John on SR 23.

Paddling to Bonnie Lake

This destination is cited by many paddlers as high on their list of "someday" trips they're going to take. Its very inaccessibility is one attraction of this beautiful lake, located close to 30 miles south of Spokane. But equally compelling is the scenery along the route you must paddle to reach the lake, as well as the beautiful, isolated setting of the lake itself.

As mentioned above, access to Bonnie Lake is by way of Rock Creek, which flows from north to south through the Hole in the Ground, a flood channel found between Bonnie Lake to the north and Rock Lake to the south. Paddling up the sluggish creek for about 1 mile is actually quite a fun and unique adventure, certainly not the typical way in which paddlers put in at a lake. The steep basalt walls are a striking backdrop to the green, meadowlike canyon floor that you paddle through to reach Bonnie Lake.

The lake itself is in many ways like Fishtrap Lake: very narrow and flanked by high basalt walls several hundred feet above you. You can never see the entire lake at one time due to its narrow width and bends in the canyon walls. It almost feels as if you are negotiating a river, not a lake.

Although this trip can be made in a half day, an island in the middle of Bonnie Lake is owned by the Department of Natural Resources and open for overnight camping. For more details, see *Paddle Routes of the Inland Northwest* (see Recommended Resources).

6 SPRAGUE LAKE

GETTING THERE: Take I-90 to about 34 miles south of Spokane and take exit 245, then head south on SR 23 to Poplar Street in 0.2 mile. Turn right on Poplar; go another

The first time I set eyes on Sprague Lake was on a frigid, windy day in December many years ago. I was moving to the Spokane area from Portland and passing through the

0.2 mile and turn left (south) on B Street. Go yet another 0.2 mile and turn right onto First Street (which turns into Max Harder Road at the Y at the west end of the city limits). Turn left at the Y and drive west on Max Harder Road out of Sprague for 2.7 miles. At this point, turn right into the Lincoln County fishing access to Sprague Lake.

To visit another fishing area on the lake, continue southwest on Max Harder Road (which becomes Danekas Road in Adams County) to a Washington Department of Fish and Wildlife (WDFW) public fishing sign at 3.8 miles from the Y. Turn right and go 0.3 mile north, then turn left at the fork. A pullout offers an overlook of Harper Island and the surrounding bay.

REGULATIONS: Discover Pass required at access areas

last lonely stretches of the barren scablands before reaching the forested terrain closer to Spokane. The steely gray surface of this lonely body of water was frozen that day, or close to it. Blowing white flakes danced around the tumbled piles of rough basalt along its shore, while the shake roof of an abandoned cabin on the lake's sole island was slowly turning white with snow.

Six-mile-long Sprague Lake is 36 miles southwest of Spokane, nestled right below I-90 and south of the town of Sprague. The lake is surrounded by a ragged topography of sharp-edged basalt, buttes, bluffs, potholes, and small marshy ponds and lakes. At 1,900 feet in elevation, Sprague Lake is frequently frozen and snow-covered in winter. It's also shallow—not more than 28 feet at its deepest point. The reason the lake never got any deeper was because of the broad area of terrain over which ice-age floodwaters could spread out, rather than excavating a deep trench as at Rock Lake, some 16 miles to the east.

If past events can bestow a region with a present-day aura, then perhaps the sensations one gets near Sprague Lake may stem from the time of its violent creation. Thousands of years ago, one by one, columnar blocks of basalt were plucked and carried away from here by a rapid flow of water estimated by geologists to have been 8 miles wide and more than 200 feet deep. The weathered condition of basalt columns located above the rest area along the interstate hints of multiple floods over many thousands of years.

The Sprague Lake area always looks lonely, isolated, and somehow forlorn, even at the height of summer, with families in vans passing by on I-90 as they travel to and from the Spokane area on vacation. Despite its lost and lonely appearance, the lake boasts a full-service fishing and camping resort. The parklike grounds and giant cottonwoods offer a shady respite from the blazing sun

Sprague Lake under forbidding skies

in summer months. Local anglers know the lake for its trout, crappies, perch, and even bass. The lake is less visited by high-speed boaters than by small fishing boats, but it can still get busy during fishing seasons, so plan your paddle trip so it doesn't coincide with opening-day crowds.

7 ESCURE RANCH RECREATION AREA

GETTING THERE: Take I-90 to Sprague at exit 245. Turn left at the stop sign onto SR 23 and travel south for 12.2 miles to Davis Road. Turn right onto Davis Road and at 4 miles reach a Y. Stay to the right, continuing south for 3 miles to George Knott Road. Turn left onto George Knott Road and travel for 2.1 miles to the Rock Creek

Over the years, I've discovered that certain songs on my car's audio system seem to go with certain landscapes. As you bounce down the pock-marked 2-mile gravel road leading to the Escure Ranch Recreation Area (about 15 miles south of Sprague), nothing sounds better than cowboy music, from Chet Atkins to the 1970s country-rock tunes of the Marshall Tucker Band.

Part of the reason is the fact that a whole cluster of ranch structures stand intact at the

BLM public land access. Follow the BLM access road until it ends in about 2 miles. A parking area is located near Rock Creek. Ask the Spokane office of the BLM (see chapter 3) for their Escure Ranch brochure, which features a detailed map of the area and its trails.

REGULATIONS: No camping, occasional road closure during periods of fire danger

trailheads here. These buildings are empty now, but they once served as a center for both sheep and cattle ranching enterprises. The mostly tin-covered buildings, just a short walk from the parking area, are less ghostly than they are a wonderfully fitting backdrop for a day of hiking and exploring the Rock Creek canyon and its environs.

But there's more than ranch buildings to promote that Old West feel. The atmosphere is further advanced by the towering buttes, meandering creek, and winding trails—many of them former four-wheel-drive roads—that conspire to make it seem as though you have just stepped into a John Wayne movie. You can explore this BLM-operated recreation area—all 20 square miles of it—on foot, by mountain bike, or on horseback, which might be an ideal mode of transportation given the scenery that seems to have been plucked straight out of a 1950s classic western.

Trails will take you to a waterfall on Rock Creek, a few small lakes with basalt cliffs in place of shorelines, and marshy areas that invite both mammal and avian wildlife. Keep in the back of your mind the fact that rattlesnakes are not unheard of here, and watch your step if you're exploring during the summer months.

A day at Escure Ranch will leave you wanting to slap an old John Wayne movie in your DVD player when you get home. Or at least hum along with a cowboy song on your drive back to civilization.

Towell Falls Hike

One of the most scenic and enjoyable hikes at the Escure Ranch Recreation Area begins at the parking area and heads almost due south, following the course of Rock Creek for more than 1 mile before veering away somewhat and climbing toward higher ground. During the spring and fall months, when fire danger is not an issue, this old ranch road leading to scenic Towell Falls can be negotiated with a high-clearance vehicle, saving you the 3-mile hike (6 miles round-trip). It's also a great route for mountain biking. If you do it on foot, be prepared for some steep climbs, annoying flies, and occasional patches of knee-high underbrush on some sections.

The trail is well worth these minor annoyances for its variety of scenery at every bend of the road. Some stretches offer dramatic views of Rock Creek and surrounding basalt cliffs in the distance. Other parts bring you right up close to the rocky talus of buttes that tower a few hundred feet above you and shade the road for 100 yards or more. These are especially welcome sections on summer days when temperatures in the 90s and higher are not uncommon.

At the end of the old four-wheel-drive road waits your reward: a cascading tumble of white water called Towell Falls. These lovely falls are some 15 or 16 feet high and probably 25 to 30 feet across. After a hot, dry, dusty 3-mile trek, the sight of so much cold, clear water is refreshing. The only trouble with Rock Creek at this idyllic spot is the lack of any convenient access for hikers with hot, tired feet. I sincerely believed my reward for that 3-mile hike on a July day in the upper 80s was to be a soak in the cool water of the stream, but it would have required climbing through the reeds, bushes, and slippery bunchgrass that lined the banks of the creek, then hopping around on one foot while pulling off each boot, since there was no convenient place to sit down. My desire for a dip remained unfulfilled.

Turtle Lake Loop Trail

A second pleasant hike at Escure Ranch is a 5-mile loop that takes you by Turtle Lake, a small *kolk* lake. The trail begins by crossing the old wooden

Old fencing and buildings at Escure Ranch; the only thing missing is John Wayne.

bridge that fords Rock Creek, passing among the abandoned ranch buildings, then through a gate and north on an old four-wheel-drive trail that passes around some ragged scabland buttes and alongside a series of wetlands with small ponds and plenty of western atmosphere. Deer are numerous here; look for them atop the piles of talus beneath the columnar basalt of the many buttes. In the small cavities near the top of one basalt butte live a flock of cliff swallows; watch and listen for this busy community as you round the prominent butte.

8 STAIRCASE RAPIDS

GETTING THERE: From I-90 at Ritzville, head south (or from Washtucna, go north) on SR 261. From the north, turn east after about 17 miles onto unpaved Sutton Road. From Washtucna, Sutton is about 8 miles north. Continuing 2 miles to Snyder Road, turn right (south). Go 1 mile to reach the end of the road and the beginning of the trail.

Spectacular geologic features in the scablands, such as Dry Falls, Potholes Coulee, and Palouse Falls, are popular destinations for anyone wanting a look at the cataclysmic floods' dramatic effects on rock and earth. To get a complete picture of the terrain, however, some of the lesser-known geologic sites in the scablands should be visited as well, though they may be less spectacular than the more publicized attractions.

Of the many fantastic remnants of swift-flowing flood pathways in eastern Washington's scablands region, Staircase Rapids is one of the most fascinating. This is a place where floodwaters rushed down a steeply sloping piece of land toward the Palouse River at an estimated 70 miles per hour. It is also near the point where the floods gained so much energy that they rerouted the Palouse, or "captured" it, as geologists like to say, and sent the river crashing through a divide, then carved a rugged canyon down to the Snake River.

Staircase Rapids consists of a series of basalt cliffs or high ridges that descend like stairs between Rattlesnake Flat on the north and Washtucna

A hiker looks over the lip of the dry falls at Staircase Rapids.

Coulee to the south. The rapids were defined on both sides by Palouse hills, all of them streamlined and scarped by the floodwaters. These steeply sloped hills are almost bullet shaped, their aerodynamic form created by swiftly flowing water on both sides.

Geologist J Harlen Bretz observed these scarped hills and theorized that glacial floods had dropped 300 feet in elevation over just 6 miles! You can take SR 261 south from Ritzville for about 18 miles and reach a point where the basalt cliffs that once were the rapids can be seen to the east. Or you can take a trail to the rapids themselves.

From the trailhead it's just 0.4 mile to the top of the upper rapids. Stroll along the precipice to the east, and you'll enjoy some great views from the top of the rapids. Remember, the property owners have agreed to allow the public access to this significant geologic area on their land, so please respect their property rights. Please do not litter or trespass into the nearby fields of crops.

9 PALOUSE FALLS AND CANYON

GETTING THERE: From the junction of SR 26 and SR 261 at Washtucna, drive southwest on SR 261 about 6 miles to the junction with

Among the scablands' most visited locales, Palouse Falls State Park is nonetheless off the beaten path and a bit of a drive. The key attraction of this park, of course, is the

SR 260, then turn left at the grain elevator. Follow SR 261 southeast for just under 9 miles to Palouse Falls Road. Turn left and take the road to its end, about 2.5 miles.
REGULATIONS: State park fees may apply.

dramatic vista of the waterfall, which—unlike most falls—is not viewed from its base, looking up, but from above, from the opposite side of the colossal semicircular amphitheater into which the water plunges nearly 200 feet.

Thousands of years ago, during the height of ice-age flooding, the falls were equal in magnitude to the wide lip and vast plunge pool that remain. It was the small size of the contemporary falls in comparison with the huge basalt amphitheater that led J Harlen Bretz to deduce that only a cataclysmic flood could have created this scene. Today, the falls vary in width depending on the time of year and flow of the Palouse River, but their height is just shy of 200 feet.

The thundering cascade of water is the key attraction here, but if you turn your gaze away from the falls and look south, an equally dramatic view of the Palouse River canyon comes into sight. A series of bends in the carved basalt river channel make for a breathtaking vista of the multilayered lava flows that were exposed when the ice-age floods poured through here. In winter, ice coats the cliffs from the spray of the falls. In spring, grass, lichen, and small plants cling to the ledges that separate each band of basalt, creating an Eden-like oasis through which the Palouse River winds lazily toward the Snake River. The diminutive flow of the river—really little more than a creek here—more than exposes the impossibility of this monumental canyon having been formed by this languid little stream.

A third attraction at Palouse Falls State Park is the short hiking trail that leads to upper Palouse Canyon above the falls. There is no safe way to hike down to the bottom of the falls, though a few faint trails appear to do just that. Chain-link fences line the gorge for several hundred feet in either direction of the main viewing area. Danger signs and barricades also make it more difficult to tumble over the edge if you are observing basic safety precautions. Then again, there's something about staring down at thousands of gallons of falling water that makes a person tend to start leaning forward

Dramatic Palouse Falls overlook

and following the descent of all that cool, splashing water into the gorge below. So just be careful, OK?

If you approach Palouse Canyon from the Snake River side, it is possible to hike all the way up the canyon to the base of the falls. You can also paddle upriver from the Snake. The stunning canyon scenery here will make it difficult to keep your mind on negotiating the river, but there *is* some work to be done both upstream and down.

Paddling to the Base of Palouse Falls

No, I'm not suggesting you go over the 200-foot falls in your kayak, as one foolhardy daredevil did in 2010. The dramatic video is probably still floating around the internet somewhere. What I am suggesting is a 6.5-mile paddle up the Palouse River from its junction with the Snake River to the base of Palouse Falls. The reward at the end of your three-hour paddle (one-way) is the dramatic sight of Palouse Falls from its base, a view not available from the state park facilities up top.

Much of the Palouse River canyon was inundated in 1969 when the Lower Monumental Dam was built on the Snake River about 15 miles to the west. This makes for a long stretch of flat water, but upstream from the flooded area there are sections of low water, a series of small rapids, and other occasional obstacles that must be negotiated or portaged around. The brush is thick on both sides of the river, and, depending what time of the year you visit (February through May is best), you may be pestered by ticks, poison ivy, and the ever-present rattlesnakes that frequent the area. For more detailed information, see *Paddle Routes of the Inland Northwest* (see Recommended Resources).

10 WASHTUCNA COULEE

GETTING THERE: From I-90 at Ritzville, take SR 261 south for about 25 miles to the town of Washtucna. Continue west another 30 miles on SR 260, through the coulee to Connell, on US 395. You can also head south from Ritzville on US 395 for about 50 miles to Connell, then turn east on SR 260 into the coulee and head "upstream" to view Washtucna Coulee's 30-mile length.

Washtucna is a great coulee to drive through because it has not been overly developed or farmed, which provides for a scenic 30-mile drive through terrain that hasn't changed for thousands of years. It also happens to be the best route to reach a number of other interesting flood features that surround the coulee on all sides.

Washtucna Coulee was a major route for floodwaters that flowed down through the Cheney-Palouse Scabland tract. The coulee was carved by the floods, but the Palouse River had originally created the much more subtly shaped river valley that once existed here. Today, Washtucna Coulee is a ragged-edged, dry trench with 200- to 300-foot basalt walls rising above its arid, basalt-strewn channel bed.

Washtucna Coulee also played a significant role in J Harlen Bretz's growing understanding of the mechanics of ice-age flooding. When he and a handful of graduate students first explored the coulee on foot, they noted scabland features atop the plateau above the coulee's 300-foot walls. They also saw that water had risen above the coulee's walls to carve out Devils Canyon clear down to the Snake River. Just east of the coulee's beginnings near the town of Washtucna, they could see how floodwaters had so overwhelmed the Palouse River that they had, in effect, captured that river and rerouted it.

Bretz knew that the volume of water, its depth, and its speed were factors in causing it to climb above the divide that lay between the southern wall of Washtucna Coulee and the Snake River about 5–10 miles south, running roughly parallel to the coulee. But it was in Washtucna Coulee that he began to wonder if there might be other factors in play.

Later, after seeing Wallula Gap (or Gateway, as Bretz called it) and realizing how this narrow passageway had served to back up floodwaters into a huge lake, he began to see how this backup of water might have lent a hand in the formation of Devils Canyon and the rerouting of the Palouse. Bretz theorized that the backup of water behind Wallula Gap was so great that it began to fill Washtucna Coulee from the southwest. The coulee, then, was being filled from both its east and west sides. As a result, there was so much water in Washtucna Coulee that water levels topped the divide and the excess water flowed over at two places: the area now occupied by Palouse Canyon and the channel now called Devils Canyon.

The road through Washtucna Coulee

This realization marked a major point in Bretz's development of his evolving flood theories over a dozen years of field research. And Washtucna Coulee represents an ideal opportunity for those of us exploring the Channeled Scablands today to see the same flood features seen by Bretz and to better appreciate not only his theory but also the processes he went through to arrive at his then-radical hypothesis.

The 30-mile road through Washtucna Coulee varies from a route along the floor of the coulee to one that hugs the north wall, to a road that rises up and above the southern wall toward the final few miles to the coulee's mouth. The change in position of the road allows you to see the effects of the floods from different vantage points, all of them offering spectacular views. Access points to Palouse Falls (#9), Devils Canyon (#11), and Esquatzel Coulee (#38, in chapter 8) are all gained by taking a drive through Washtucna Coulee. Part of the Columbia Plateau Trail (see sidebar), for hikers and bikers, follows Washtucna Coulee for about 13 miles until turning south through Devils Canyon.

11 DEVILS CANYON

GETTING THERE: From the junction of US 395 and SR 260 at Connell, drive east on SR 260 for 14 miles to SR 263 at Kahlotus (about 13 miles west of Washtucna). At Kahlotus, head south on Pasco-Kahlotus Road for about 0.5 mile to the junction with SR 263. Follow Pasco-Kahlotus Road to the right, then almost immediately pull out to an open area on your

When floodwaters that created the Cheney-Palouse Scabland reached the area north of present-day Washtucna, they encountered the westward-tracking Palouse River. At that time, this little river flowed west through a gently sloped valley that veered south at a point near today's Connell, then directed the river into the what is now the Tri-Cities area, where the Palouse entered the Columbia somewhere near the present city of Pasco.

left. From here you can see the head of Devils Canyon.

When the massive wall of water that was the Glacial Lake Missoula flood hit the Palouse River, it poured up and over the east-west divide separating the Palouse from the Snake River, tearing away at the soil and the basalt beneath that soil to carve out the Palouse Canyon and create Palouse Falls.

But much of the floodwaters followed the natural route of the Palouse through that gentle valley, carving it into the east-west trench we know today as Washtucna Coulee. Even when it had been carved into a deep, U-shaped channel, Washtucna Coulee still could not hold all the floodwaters that entered it, and the water rose up the south wall until it broke through and over a low spot, then raced south to the Snake River at a point where the Lower Monumental Dam now stands.

The gash in the southern wall of Washtucna Coulee and the narrow corridor leading down to the Snake River are now called Devils Canyon, just south of Kahlotus. The steeply dropping viaduct for ancient floodwaters now runs for about 4 miles and drops several hundred feet in elevation before reaching the Snake River. At a pullout at the head of the canyon, you can see the last cliff edges to be left behind when the final drops of water ran down this route. Be careful if you hike down to the edge of these dry

Midway through Devils Canyon, looking south

falls. In some respects, these drop-offs are frozen in time, looking just as they would have on that last significant day when the water stopped running some 15,000 years ago.

An abruptly descending paved road—Devils Canyon Road—allows you to drive down to the Snake River, where a massive sand and gravel bar reveals the amount of earthen material that was repeatedly dumped by the flow of water that entered the Snake River here. The Columbia Plateau Trail (see sidebar) also passes through Devils Canyon on the west side, allowing hikers and bikers to gaze across at the east side of the basalt channel and see the fascinating columnar structure that formed over millions of years.

Columbia Plateau Trail

Park at the pullout along Devils Canyon Road about 1.6 miles south of the pullout above at the head of the canyon. Cut across-canyon to connect with the trail, about 100 feet to the west. You can hike north or south on the trail; either direction takes you through a dark railway tunnel—bring a flashlight.

COLUMBIA PLATEAU TRAIL STATE PARK

One unique aspect of the Cheney-Palouse Scabland tract is the presence of a 130-mile trail passing right through the region from the north, starting near Cheney, to the south, ending on the Snake River near Pasco. The Columbia Plateau Trail is a combined hiking, biking, and equestrian trail that utilizes an abandoned rail line passing through some of the most geologically significant and scenic parts of the scablands.

The trail passes close to many of the scabland locations described in this chapter, among them Fish Lake (#1), Turnbull National Wildlife Refuge (#2), Escure Ranch (#7), Washtucna Coulee (#10), and Devils Canyon (#11). The trail (when completely opened) will also pass through lengthy tunnels and across towering trestles while offering spectacular vistas of scabland buttes, pothole lakes, columnar basalt, and flood-scoured Palouse hills. Some of the most scenic parts along the Columbia Plateau Trail include the Cow Creek Trestle, Devils Canyon, and the Little Palouse Falls (near SR 26 a few miles east of Washtucna). The abandoned railroad corridor itself offers fascinating historical artifacts including tunnels, trestles, reservoir flumes, and the foundations of homes, stations, and other railroad properties.

The Spokane, Portland, and Seattle Railway Company built the railroad during the 1900s. It is said that the "Seattle" in the name was there only to mislead competing companies at a time when railroad tracks were being laid throughout the region, some might say at an excessive rate. Intense competition among railroad companies in the early twentieth century meant that the speed with which lines were completed was all important. For this reason, trestles were initially built to carry trains over flood channels and other deep gaps in the terrain. Trestles were generally considered to be temporary structures, because they were quick to build and helped railroad companies finish their line in time. But trestles also were subject to deterioration from weather and often caught fire. After the rail lines were established, the company could then hire laborers—frequently Chinese immigrants—to haul crushed rock and earth by wheelbarrow and painstakingly cover the foundations of the trestles, some of them 100 feet high or more, with huge mounds of dirt and rock.

The rail line ran until 1987, when it ceased operation forever. Washington State Parks acquired it four years later, with a plan to convert it into a multi-use recreational trail corridor. In 1995 the State Parks joined with the US Fish and Wildlife Service to manage the part of the trail that bisects the Turnbull National Wildlife Refuge. The Cheney to Fish Lake section of the trail is a blacktop surface, but the rest is crushed rock, and unimproved stretches were built with extremely large and sharp-edged rocks, a challenge even for top-of-the-line mountain bikes. Over time, these larger rocks will be broken down into more accommodating crushed-rock trail surfaces.

Although most of the trail can be accessed at spots where the old rail line crosses state highways and county roads throughout the region, many parts of the trail are considered closed because of dangerous trestles, lack of side rails through steep canyons, unimproved trail surfaces, or hazards. The trail often crosses huge fills of earth and basalt rocks that span numerous deep flood channels along the route of the former SPSRC track. What is *not* visible are the huge wooden trestles that lie beneath the fill materials.

A blacktopped section of the Columbia Plateau Trail, near Cheney

In most cases, both sides of the trail corridor are private property, and trail rangers ask that hikers, bikers, and equestrians respect the property rights of the owners. They also remind people thinking of exploring the more isolated parts of the 130-mile trail that services are nonexistent, temperatures can be extreme, and—for some unknown reason—rattlesnakes seem to love hanging out along railway corridors.

The entire Columbia Plateau Trail is not open for travel. To find out which sections are open, call or visit one of the two Trail offices, in Cheney or Washtucna (see below). The best way to see different sections of the trail is to park at various trailheads along the entire 130-mile route and hike a few miles in either direction, then get back in your vehicle and proceed to another trailhead. (Note: A Discover Pass is required to park at trailheads.) To check trail conditions before planning a hike or bike trip, call Washington State Parks (360-902-8844). To obtain a map of the entire trail, contact one of the two Columbia Plateau Trail offices: 15 Union Street, Cheney, WA 99004, (509) 235-4696; and 100 SW Main Street, Washtucna, WA 99371, (509) 646-9218; CPT.Central@Parks.wa.gov.

CHENEY-PALOUSE SCABLAND AUTO TOURS

There is much to see within the Cheney-Palouse Scabland tract, and these two suggested day-long drives could easily be extended to a couple of days or more, depending on the amount of time you have and what scabland features you'd like to visit. Directions offered here are minimal; as you read about each suggested destination on these trips, refer to the descriptions in this chapter about that specific destination, where more detailed directions are provided.

 CHENEY-AREA LAKES LOOP

The Cheney-Palouse Lakes Loop takes you past a number of flood-created *kolk* lakes and other geologic features in a one-day loop trip, starting and ending in Cheney. It's a great introduction to how scabland lakes were formed and what they look like now, thousands of years after the last flood event. The following 100-mile day-long trip in the scabland region south of Cheney can also be shortened to a half-day 45-mile loop.

Fish Lake: Start from Cheney by taking the Cheney-Spokane Road north to see Fish Lake, just about 3.5 miles north of town. There is a nice Spokane County Park here, and you can also take a look at the Fish Lake trailhead of the Columbia Plateau Trail (see the sidebar) at a point where it is smooth, flat, and blacktopped.

Turnbull National Wildlife Refuge: Return to Cheney and head south on Main Street (SR 904) to the junction with Cheney-Plaza Road. Take this road south from Cheney about 4 miles and watch for signs to the Turnbull National Wildlife Refuge. Enjoy the refuge's visitor center and take the 5.5-mile auto tour route, which is open year-round.

Rock Creek Overlook: Leaving Turnbull, continue south on Cheney-Plaza Road about 5 miles and turn left at a sign for Chapman Lake. Look to your right and pull over for a view of the small canyon where Rock Creek flows east, then south into Bonnie Lake. This canyon pretty much begins out of nowhere; geologists believe that an ancient fault line captured floodwaters during the Glacial Lake Missoula floods and created a major pathway for the floods that eventually carved out Bonnie Lake (out of sight about 4 miles to the south), Hole in the Ground (another 5 miles south), and Rock Lake (about 8 miles away).

Williams and Badger Lakes: Returning to Cheney-Plaza Road, turn left and continue south to Williams Lake Road, another 1.5 miles down the road. Turn right on Williams Lake Road and drive just over 2 miles to Badger Lake Road. Turn right on to this road, then pull off to the right and park. Carefully watching for traffic, walk across the road and head on foot across the rocky plateau toward the lip of the 100-foot dry fall that lies between Badger and Williams lakes. Depending on the time of the year, there may be a few small streams running across this plateau, and you may need to jump across these or there may be a makeshift board bridge to walk across. As you approach the lip of the dry falls, you encounter a wonderful view to the southwest. From the top you can see the remains of the semicircular lip of the falls heading in either direction, about 0.25 mile in width overall. Directly below you is the talus pile formed by basalt that has crumbled from the edge and tumbled over the side during the last 15,000 years or so since the last flood passed over the falls. About 0.5 mile away is Williams Lake. When floodwaters raced through here multiple times thousands of years ago, great waterfalls formed west of here and receded each time there was a flood, until the falls finally stopped flowing at this spot.

Returning to your vehicle, continue down Badger Lake Road about 1.5 miles to see the south end of Badger Lake, where there is a public boat launch and a small trailer park community. Please observe all posted rules regarding parking and vehicle speed. Returning to Williams Lake Road, continue west (right), and you will shortly drop down into the basalt-lined hollow where Williams Lake lies. After you have dropped down the hill and the road makes a turn to the right, look for a wide spot where you can pull over for a good view to your right of the dry falls you stood atop a short while earlier. Continuing down the road less than 1 mile, reach a turnoff to the left leading into a small trailer park community at Williams Lake, similar to the one at Badger Lake. Here you'll find a boat launch, a small swimming area, and a gourmet restaurant called Klink's. If you have arrived here around lunchtime, it's a great place to stop for a bite.

At this point, you can cut your Cheney-Area Lakes Loop to a half day by continuing west on Williams Lake Road about 1.5 miles to Mullinix Road, then turning right on Mullinix and heading north back to Cheney for a scenic back-road drive about 12 miles long. Total mileage of this shorter loop is about 45 miles.

Rock Lake and Environs: To continue, from Williams Lake head back east on Williams Lake Road 2 miles, retracing your drive to Cheney-Plaza Road, which changes its name at this point to Rock Lake Road. Continue south just over 5 miles and turn left on gravel Miller Road. After a little less than 1 mile, veer left onto gravel Belsby Road. After about 3 miles, this road begins dropping into a deep coulee, Hole in the Ground. At the bottom of the switchbacks, you reach the bottom of this deep, flood-carved channel and a bridge across Rock Creek. This is a good place to get some photos looking north or south into this dry-land zone between Bonnie Lake to the north and Rock Lake to the south. Pull your vehicle well to the side of the road, since cars, trucks, and farm equipment use this road frequently.

Retrace your route to Rock Lake Road via Belsby and Miller Roads. The quickest way to get a look at Rock Lake is to continue south on Rock Lake Road about 8 miles to the southern end of the lake, where there is a gravel parking lot and boat launch. Rock Lake's high basalt cliffs are less impressive here than farther north, but you'll get an idea of the size of this lake.

Sprague Lake: Continue south on Rock Lake Road just under 2 miles to the junction with SR 23. Head west on this road for about 19 miles to Sprague. Watch for the terrain to change from rugged scabland basalt to rich farmland and back again as you head west toward Sprague. At Sprague, drive south either along I-90, which follows the west side of Sprague Lake, or through town and along Danekas Road, which travels along the east side of the lake (see #6, Getting There).

Fishtrap–Hog Lake Recreation Area: Return to the town of Sprague and head north 8 miles on I-90, then take exit 254 and follow signs to Fishtrap Lake, about 3 miles. If it's late spring or summer and the dirt back roads are passable, take a look at beautiful Hog Lake as well.

Return to I-90, continue north and take exit 257 (Cheney-Tyler), then head back into Cheney, another 10 miles. Total mileage of this longer loop is about 100 miles.

PALOUSE–SNAKE RIVER LOOP

This one-day 140-mile trip takes you south from Ritzville all the way to the Snake River and back, visiting several dramatic flood features along the way.

Staircase Rapids: From I-90 at Ritzville, take SR 261 south 17 miles to Sutton Road, follow it 2 miles to Snyder Road, then turn right on Snyder and follow that 1 mile to Staircase Rapids, the dry remains of a once-dramatic series of cascades rushing downslope toward the Palouse River at an estimated 70 miles per hour. The parking area and short hike are on private land that the landowner has agreed to let visitors use to view Staircase Rapids. Please stay on the trail and respect the property owner's rights.

Palouse Falls and Canyon: Return 1 mile to Sutton Road, head west 2 miles back to SR 261, then south about 8 miles to the town of Washtucna. At Washtucna, follow SR 260 west just under 6 miles to a turnoff south onto SR 261 and a sign directing you to Palouse Falls State Park. About 12 miles farther on SR 261, turn off to the left at signs for the park. In another 2 miles you enter the state park, and the road takes you to a parking area to view the falls and canyon.

Devils Canyon: Return 2 miles to SR 261, then 12 miles north to SR 260 in Washtucna Coulee; turn left (west) on SR 260 and drive about 7 miles to Kahlotus. At Kahlotus, head south on Pasco-Kahlotus Road. At a point about 0.5 mile up this road, it divides. Follow Pasco-Kahlotus Road to the right, then almost immediately pull out to an open area on your left. From here you can see the head of Devils Canyon and the abrupt lip of the cascades that flowed here until the end of the last flood some 15,000 years ago. Return to the fork and take the other road—SR 263—down through Devils Canyon to its junction with the Snake River in about 5 miles. You can see a large flood bar on the east side of the highway just as you make the turn at the mouth of the canyon. At the Lower Monumental Dam on the Snake River, turn around and retrace your route. On your way back up Devils Canyon, look high up on the walls of the east side for uniquely twisted or warped columns of basalt.

Washtucna Coulee: Return north on SR 263 to Kahlotus and head west through Washtucna Coulee on SR 260 about 17 miles to Connell, on US 395. Washtucna Coulee was originally the conduit west for the Palouse River, until ice-age floodwaters rerouted the Palouse. Picture Washtucna Coulee filled to the brim with floodwaters that flowed from east to west here and topped the coulee walls to create Devils Canyon, which you just visited.

Return to Ritzville by driving about 40 miles north on US 395 to I-90. Total mileage is 140 miles.

FIVE

Telford–Crab Creek Tract

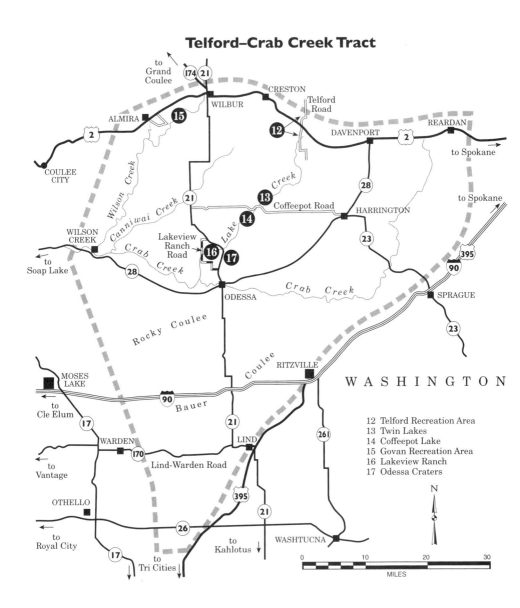

to Grand Coulee

174 21

CRESTON

WILBUR

Telford Road

15

ALMIRA

12

DAVENPORT

REARDAN

2

2

to Spokane

COULEE CITY

Wilson Creek

Creek

to Spokane

21

13

Coffeepot Road

28

14

HARRINGTON

WILSON CREEK

Canniwai Creek

Lake

Lakeview Ranch Road

16

17

23

to Soap Lake

Crab Creek

28

Crab Creek

ODESSA

SPRAGUE

Rocky Coulee

395

90

23

MOSES LAKE

Coulee

RITZVILLE

WASHINGTON

90

Bauer

to Cle Elum

17

21

261

WARDEN

170

LIND

12 Telford Recreation Area
13 Twin Lakes
14 Coffeepot Lake
15 Govan Recreation Area
16 Lakeview Ranch
17 Odessa Craters

to Vantage

Lind-Warden Road

OTHELLO

395

21

N

to Royal City

26

WASHTUCNA

17

to Tri Cities

to Kahlotus

0   10   20   30

MILES

Opposite page: *Lakeview Ranch corral area*

TELFORD–CRAB CREEK TRACT

Perhaps nowhere else in the Channeled Scablands can you see the dramatic and often immediate contrast between farmland and scabland as vividly as within the Telford–Crab Creek Tract. This tract of scabland mixed with farmland ranges from 20 to 70 miles wide and is about 70 miles long.

Along stretches of US 2—notably, between Davenport and Almira—rich farmland is bisected regularly by abrupt strips of ragged basalt. This scabland features harsh-looking native plants that can tolerate the thin, poor soil so unlike the rich loess of the Palouse Hills where lush crops of wheat, alfalfa, and seed oil grains are grown. Similar contrasting views of agriculturally rich land sliced by rough, unproductive tracts of scabland can be found north of Odessa, south of Harrington, and other spots along the half dozen or so paved highways that traverse this region. Rocky and Bauer coulees can be seen from SR 21 south of Odessa.

This tract of scabland has many small creeks and streams flowing through enlarged U-shaped channels formed when ice-age floods followed the routes of existing streams and dramatically deepened and widened these routes. Examples of small streams flowing through wide, impressive channels are Wilson Creek, Canniwai Creek, Goose Creek, and Sinking Creek, among others.

Strings of *kolk* lakes are interspersed by generally sluggish little streams throughout the Telford–Crab Creek Tract. The Lake Creek Corridor (see below) is the longest of these chains of lakes, containing Twin and Coffepot lakes, as well as the various lakes in the Lakeview Ranch Recreation Area.

The Telford–Crab Creek Tract of scabland is also the site of strange, craterlike formations found nowhere else on earth but in the Channeled Scablands. More than 100 of these craters are near Odessa, and short hikes allow you to see them close up.

THE LAKE CREEK FLOOD CHANNEL

The primary flood channel that travels from northeast to southwest through the Telford–Crab Creek Tract, Lake Creek begins a few miles south of Telford Recreation Area on US 2 in northern Lincoln County and flows some 23 miles to Crab Creek near Odessa. (Crab Creek begins its 163-mile

Canniwai Creek Flood Channel

journey near Reardan off US 2 and flows to the Columbia near Beverly; see chapter 7.) In Lake Creek's short 23-mile stretch, the creek is sometimes little more than a trickle, but the signs of its former strength are evident.

Along that short run south, Lake Creek flows into and out of no fewer than nineteen lakes, nearly one for each mile of its total length. Some of these are tiny lakes just a few hundred yards long. Others are 1, 2, and, in the case of Coffeepot Lake, even 3 miles in length. Most of the lakes, but especially those larger bodies of water, are *kolk* lakes that were churned into existence by the rapidly revolving funnels of water that circulated deep below the surface of floodwaters passing through here several thousand years ago.

THE LEGEND OF HARRY TRACY

They no doubt had a second press run of the *Spokesman-Review* on August 7, 1902, a day after Harry Tracy was killed in a cornfield near Creston, a small town at the northern end of the Telford–Crab Creek Tract of the Channeled Scablands.

Harry Tracy had been an outlaw in the last days of the Old West. His real name was Harry Severns, and it was said that he hung out with Butch Cassidy and the Hole in the Wall Gang. When he went on his own as an adult, he was actively committing robbery and murder. In 1901 Tracy was captured, convicted, and sent to the Oregon State Penitentiary. He managed to escape on June 9, 1902, shooting and killing corrections officers Thurston Jones Sr., Bailey Tiffany, and Frank Ferrell as well as three civilians.

Perhaps the most famous thing about Tracy was the size and scope of the manhunt that searched for him, not to mention the extensive, for its time, media coverage. He evaded capture for an entire month, mostly taking refuge in the Seattle area. On July 3, 1902, he set up an ambush near Bothell, Washington, where he killed detective Charles Raymond and deputy John Williams during a shootout.

Tracy fled, took several hostages in a residence, and engaged other law enforcement officers in a shootout. During that shootout, he killed posse members Cornelius Rowley and Enoch Breece. Tracy headed east into the little-known and sparsely settled scabland area of eastern Washington, where he hid out for nearly a month amid the basalt outcroppings and contorted landscape. A small lava cave is still called Tracy's Cave to this day.

On August 6, 1902, near Creston, Washington, Tracy was cornered and shot in the leg during an ambush by a posse from Lincoln County, resulting in his being badly wounded. Sheriff Gardner arrived, and he and his men surrounded the field that Tracy had crawled into. Harry committed suicide to avoid capture.

TOWNS IN THE TELFORD–CRAB CREEK TRACT

- ALMIRA, on US 2 west of Wilbur, was founded more than 100 years ago as settlers came to claim the good farmland they had heard about. The glory days for Almira were in the early 1930s, when the town became headquarters for the newest project of the Bureau of Reclamation: building a dam at Grand Coulee. Almira's population today is a little over 300. Services include a motel and gift shop.

- CRESTON, on US 2 between Davenport and Wilbur, sprang up with the arrival of the Central Washington Railroad in 1889. The town's name included the word "crest" because it had the highest elevation (2,436 feet) of any town between Wenatchee and Spokane, as far as the railroad goes. Creston today has about 250 residents. Services include a restaurant, gas station, RV park, and convenience store.

- DAVENPORT, on US 2 at the junction with SR 28, is one of the larger cities in Lincoln County, with a population of more than 1,700. It is also the county seat. Though flanked by scabland channels, Davenport is in the heart of productive agricultural land: Lincoln County is the world's second-largest wheat producing county. Services include motels, gas stations, small grocery stores, and a hospital.

- HARRINGTON, on SR 28 south of Davenport, is a town in Lincoln County with a population of a little more than 400. The town was named for W. P. Harrington, a banker from Colusa, California, who had heavily invested in local land. The town has many historic old brick buildings; one of these, the Harrington Opera House, has been lovingly restored and offers plays, music, speakers, and other events year-round. Other services include a grocery store and a bank.

- LIND, on SR 21 about 10 miles south of I-90, was settled in 1888 along the Northern Pacific Railway's main line. The reason for its name has been lost. By 1901, several brick buildings were being built for a bank and stores, while hundreds of temporary dwellings were constructed by settlers, mostly farmers. With just under 600 people, Lind is home to a combine demolition derby held each June. All basic services are found here, including groceries and a restaurant.

- ODESSA, at the junction of SR 28 and SR 21, is a town in Lincoln County with a population of just under 1,000 people. The original railroad siding was named Odessa Siding by railroad surveyors after the Russian city of Odessa, because many German-speaking Russian wheat farmers had settled in the area. Odessa is known for its annual Odessa Deutschesfest, a German-themed festival. Services include hotels, restaurants, and gas stations.

- REARDAN is on US 2 between Spokane and Davenport. Services include restaurants and grocery stores.

- WILBUR, at the junction of US 2 and SR 21, was the result of a post office being assigned to Samuel Wilbur Condin, and a town soon followed.

Wilbur was brought out of the hard times of the 1890s during a bountiful wheat harvest in 1897, which brought more than $1 million to invest in the town. Wilbur's population today is about 900. Services include motels and restaurants.

- WILSON CREEK, on SR 28 west of Odessa, was founded in 1903. The community has solid ties to the local agricultural economy dominating the region. Wilson Creek itself flows through a large flood channel near this town, which is also close to Billy Clapp Lake and Pinto Dam, both part of the Columbia Basin Irrigation Project. Services include a grocery store.

12 TELFORD RECREATION AREA

GETTING THERE: From Davenport on US 2, travel about 12 miles west to Telford Road. You can travel either north of the highway or south on Telford Road; either way, you are now in BLM-managed land and can enjoy hiking, dispersed camping, and hunting in season. Because BLM land here is surrounded by private property, you are urged to obtain a map of the recreation area from the Spokane BLM office (see chapter 3) or online (www.or.blm.gov/spokane).

The Telford Recreation Area, BLM public use lands off US 2 in northern Lincoln County, is undeveloped terrain that represents the way the land would have looked back in the decade of the 1920s when J Harlen Bretz wandered through here. It was in this region that he made measurements of Palouse hill "islands" and the slope of land from north to south in the Lincoln County scabland tracts.

This is not spectacularly scenic scab land terrain such as that near Palouse Falls, Grand Coulee, or Drumheller Channels, but it is representative of typical scabland landscapes: wide stretches of open, ravaged countryside with small basalt knobs and buttes and potholes in abundance.

Because most of the streams in Lincoln
County were likely already here in different forms many thousands of years ago,
their pathways—initially small, wandering
creases in the land—became the routes followed by floodwaters, which
consequently widened and deepened their channels. Instead of the dry,
wide flood channels of the Cheney-Palouse Scabland tract, where streams
never ran and do not run today, the coulees of Lincoln County are largely
the widened paths of streams such as Lake Creek, Canniwai Creek, Willow
Creek, and Crab Creek.

The Telford Recreation Area consists of about 5 square miles of land
north of and about 13 square miles south of US 2, situated about 12 miles
west of Davenport. Drive Telford Road to the north or south of the highway
to enjoy what I think of as a free-range hiking and dispersed camping experience in a raw, unimproved scabland setting. There are few well-defined trails
here; exploration of the terrain is chiefly a cross-country affair.

Lake Creek begins near here, broken along its 23-mile length by numerous lakes in typically basalt-line depressions, among them Twin Lakes,
Coffeepot Lake, and Deer Lake, all farther south.

An abandoned homestead near Coffeepot Lake

13 TWIN LAKES RECREATION AREA

GETTING THERE: From US 2 at Davenport, travel south via SR 28 to Harrington, then turn west on Coffeepot Road and drive about 12 miles to Highline Road; turn right on Highline and watch for the Twin Lakes access road sign at the 1.5-mile mark. From US 2 at Wilbur, take SR 21 south about 19 miles to Eagle Spring Road and follow this east about 5 miles, where it changes to Coffeepot Road; follow Coffeepot Road east about 6 miles to Highline Road, turn left onto it, and watch for the Twin Lakes access road at about 1.5 miles.

From either approach, follow the unpaved access road for about 2 miles. This dirt road is reasonably smooth and maintained in summer months, but be prepared for large puddles of water, potholes, and very soft surfaces after heavy rains or in spring after a lot of snowmelt. Also,

One of the most scenic of the lakes along Lake Creek is Twin Lakes, actually two deep, narrow *kolk* lakes laid out in the typical northeast-to-southwest pattern along the Lake Creek flood channel. The two lakes are linked by a narrow isthmus where the creek flows from the upper lake to the lower. Together, the upper and lower lakes are a little more than 2 miles in length.

Steep basalt cliffs line both sides of both the upper and lower lakes, and north of the upper lake the canyon created by these cliffs continues, accessible by hiking cross-country or via a few faint trails. The spectacular scenery of rock formations, pools, and wetlands within the walls of this canyon are worth a hike to view. This canyon's relative inaccessibility makes it all the more special, and the solitude is a precious commodity.

Between the two arms of Twin Lakes is a pleasant camping and grassy picnicking area, a boat launch, and restrooms. This mixed use recreation area includes the lake and more than 14,000 acres of BLM land surrounding it. The best way to get a feel for the surroundings here is to take all or part of the 9.5-mile loop trail that starts between the two sections of lake and loops the last 0.1 mile consists of a few sharp switchbacks and is fairly steep; it may be difficult to negotiate if towing a trailer or a mobile home. The BLM Spokane office (see chapter 3) offers a helpful map and brochure about Twin Lakes.

REGULATIONS: No hunting

around the high country towering above these bodies of water. Another two dozen or more trails and abandoned dirt roads can be followed to smaller pothole lakes, rocky outcroppings, and areas of typical shrubsteppe terrain and vegetation.

Wildlife includes a wide variety of migratory and lakeshore birds such as plovers, avocets, stilts, and greater yellowlegs. Mule deer are commonly seen in early morning hours, and reptile lovers will like the painted turtles, short-horned lizards, and at least five species of snakes found here. One of these is the western rattlesnake, so watch your step during summer months.

Twin Lakes has long been a popular recreation lake. A small resort operated there from the late 1940s into the 1960s. The BLM acquired the land in 1995. Fishing at Twin Lakes is for rainbow trout, largemouth bass, perch, bullhead, and crappie. Because these lakes are not near a major urban area like Spokane, they are much less crowded. Your experience as you explore the lakes by boat will be much quieter and the number of other people on the lake will be much less numerous.

The pleasant picnic area at Twin Lakes

Loop Trail

The 9.5-mile loop trail starts between the two sections of Twin Lakes and loops around these bodies of water. At one point, the trail drops into and passes through the northern part of the canyon tracking north from the two lakes. The canyon can also be accessed by taking the loop trail east from its start between the two lakes, then at a point about 1.5 miles from the start, take a smaller trail that connects with the loop trail and tracks north, then turns west, leading to the north end of upper Twin Lakes and the beginning of the canyon.

14 COFFEEPOT LAKE RECREATION AREA

GETTING THERE: From US 2 at Davenport, travel south via SR 28 to Harrington, turn west on Coffeepot Road, and drive about 12 miles to the Coffeepot Lake gravel access road on the left. To get a copy of the BLM brochure-map for this recreation area, contact the BLM Spokane office (see chapter 3).

REGULATIONS: No hunting

Just a few miles southwest of Twin Lakes is Coffeepot Lake, a popular recreation lake for fishing, camping, and picnicking. Coffeepot Lake offers similar scenery (with fewer trees) as many of the lakes in the Cheney-Palouse Scabland, but it is much less crowded. Like Twin Lakes, Coffeepot Lake is located in the Lake Creek flood channel and flanked by tall basalt cliffs. It is also composed of two long, narrow lakes connected by a small isthmus.

There are a few differences here, however. Unlike the Twin Lakes, Coffeepot Lake is not completely surrounded by BLM land. Bordering the west side of Coffeepot Lake is nearly all BLM, or public, land. But nearly the entire east shore is privately owned land. As a consequence, there are far fewer hiking trails here, though it is a longer and broader lake than the Twin Lakes. Coffeepot Lake has a grassy picnic area, campground, boat launch, and restrooms. This is a BLM game reserve, so no hunting is allowed.

There are no espresso stands at Coffeepot Lake.

BRETZ'S CLUES

Glacial stream runoff is a by-product of gradually melting glaciers over a long period of time. The resulting glacial stream flows across the land like any other stream or river until the glacier has completely melted. The volume of these streams can be quite great over their lifetime, but in Bretz's first scabland paper, his language came close to crediting more than glacial runoff for the scabland features he observed. Even in his first paper, Bretz concluded, "The hills which have disappeared averaged 200 feet in height and in some places the glacial torrents eroded 100 to 200 feet into the basalt. The flood originated at several places along the ice-front. Great river channels exist among the remaining hills in the flood-swept region. The area overridden by the ice itself has lost every trace of Palouse Hills." Bretz named the scabland region west of Spokane the "Crab Creek Drainage." Here, describing Telford–Crab Creek features such as the Lake Creek and Wilson Creek drainage systems as "youthful canyons in basalt," Bretz also wrote that these canyons, some of them quite deep, "are but the deepened channels of ice-born rivers, and not true valleys. Like the scablands of the Palouse region, invading but short-lived floods traversed the area."

15 GOVAN RECREATION AREA

The Govan BLM site is even smaller than the Telford Recreation Area—just over 10 square miles located south of US 2 some 5 miles east of Almira. In that 10-square-mile parcel of land, however, are dozens of pothole lakes, a few choice wildlife and wildflower observation sites, and the dramatic gash of scabland channel known as Wilson Creek.

As with the Telford site, there are few clearly defined hiking trails at Govan, with most exploration restricted to hiking or horseback riding cross-country. Enjoy these less visited scabland areas for the isolation, the freedom of hiking where you want, and the good chance of seeing wildlife and observing native plants and flowers.

A light dusting of snow in the Govan area

16 LAKEVIEW RANCH RECREATION AREA

GETTING THERE: From Odessa on SR 21, go north 2 miles to Lakeview Ranch Road, turn left, and drive 5 miles on the gravel road to Lakeview Ranch.

REGULATIONS: No motorized vehicles on many trails and roads

The southernmost section of the Lake Creek Corridor is occupied by the Lakeview Ranch Recreation Area, a BLM-administered recreation area composed largely of the former Lakeview Ranch property. As with the Escure Ranch Recreation Area south of Sprague (see chapter 4, Cheney-Palouse Scabland), abandoned ranch buildings add a feeling of the Old West to this already scenic setting in a valley flanked by towering basalt cliffs and craggy buttes.

Lakeview Ranch sits in the hollow formed by the Lake Creek flood channel, and above the ranch are rolling hills of rich farmland, where herds of mule deer often roam through the wheat fields. Lakeview Ranch is the northern terminus of the 12.5-mile Odessa to Pacific Lake Trail.

At the former ranch, the remaining corrals are in place and maintained. They are occasionally used to hold stock for wild-horse auctions and can also be used to hold trail horses overnight while their owners camp nearby. A short walk west from the ranch parking area, you can view the Lakeview Crater, a geologic feature much like those found outside of Odessa.

One regrettable change to this long-popular recreation site is the steadily lowering levels of several lakes, including Pacific Lake and Bobs Lakes, all of which were beautiful

Helpful signage and scabland terrain around Lakeview Ranch

lakes in striking basalt coulee settings and offered fishing, boating, and other waterfront activities. Large ranches in the region needed more irrigation water over the years, and deeper wells were drilled when water sources closer to the surface dried out. There have been discussions about tapping Lake Roosevelt for water to refill the dry lake basins, but as of early 2012, the lakes were still dry.

Odessa to Pacific Lake Trail

This 12.5-mile hiking trail begins in Odessa and heads north through scabland, coulee, and scenic scrub-steppe environments to Lakeview Ranch, winding around the terrain and Lake Creek flood channel. The mostly level trail is a combination of footpaths, some barely visible in places, and old four-wheel-drive trails. The mix of scenery ranges from shrub-steppe to canyon narrows to dry lakebeds. Off-road vehicles are allowed on the northern 3 miles.

17 ODESSA CRATERS

GETTING THERE: From SR 21 about 6 miles north of Odessa, look for signs indicating the Odessa Craters Loop. Park on the side of the road, and follow the trail signs. Farther up the road, just 0.25 mile or less, is a turnout for the Cache Crater Trail.

REGULATIONS: No motorized vehicles allowed on crater trails

Basaltic ring structures are enigmatic, mostly circular basalt landforms found nowhere else on Earth but in the Channeled Scablands. They were first recognized and studied in 1965 and remained the focus of geologic research through the 1970s before pretty much fading from the spotlight.

As images of landforms on Mars became increasingly available, scientists began to see similarities between features in the scablands and features on Mars. This sparked a renewed interest in the strange circular rings of basalt, sometimes with center high spots surrounded by moats. Most have craterlike depressions, which led people at first to believe these had been impact craters.

Cache Crater, north of Odessa

It appears now that the craters—more than 100 of them near Odessa—were formed as lava oozed from the ground and were compelled by an unknown series of geologic forces to attain a circular state. Like other lava flows in eastern Washington, the circular "craters" were eventually covered by topsoil and disappeared from view. It was only due to the Glacial Lake Missoula floods that these structures were exposed some 15,000 to 18,000 years ago. The Odessa Craters Loop Trail passes by three of these ring structures. Nearby is the short Cache Crater Trail, less than 0.2 mile and wheelchair accessible. It leads to the much more obvious Cache Crater, which Native Americans used to store food items.

Odessa Craters Loop Trail

The trail is about 1.5 miles in length with some minor elevation gains and drops, but it's basically an easy hike of an hour or so. Trail signs will keep you on the correct route. I will be the first to acknowledge that the ring structures are not all that easy to see. I suggest you bring a good topographic map to determine when you have come right next to one of the craters so you can distinguish it from the surrounding ragged basalt terrain. Better yet, befriend a geologist and bring him or her along.

EXPLORING WAY OUT THERE FROM WAY OUT HERE!

After thirty-two years in the Seattle area, the National UFO Reporting Center moved in 2006 to its new location in the scablands of eastern Washington: a decommissioned US Air Force intercontinental missile base, located between the towns of Davenport and Harrington on SR 28.

From the abandoned silo where a 3.75-megaton ICBM once stood ready for launching toward the Soviet Union, Peter Davenport now runs the internationally known UFO Reporting Center. The center, essentially a 24-hour hotline for sightings of unidentified flying objects, has been run by Davenport since 1994. Each year he posts as many as 5,000 sightings on ufocenter.com for all to see. He also tape-records callers and makes written reports on sightings, more than 70,000 of which he currently has on file.

Far from being one of the obsessed and slightly off-kilter individuals often associated with UFO research, Davenport is intelligent, industrious, and healthily skeptical, hardly a pushover for the thousands of alien sighting assertions he hears about every year. Davenport, who has been welcomed with open arms in the small farming town of Harrington, says that more than 90 percent of all UFO sightings reported can be chalked up to viewings of satellites, aircraft, weather balloons, or even lights on a distant airplane.

Still, he believes in the existence of alien beings and calls UFO research necessary in the pursuit to answer "the greatest scientific question that has ever confronted man." Although Davenport does not offer regular group tours of his operation, he has been known to reward anyone curious enough to seek him out with a close-up look at the reporting center facilities.

TELFORD–CRAB CREEK TRACT AUTO TOURS

To get a good overall feel for this region of scabland, the best and fastest way is to plan one or more driving tours employing a number of state and county roads, most of them paved but some gravel, which crisscross the scablands and often can be linked to create a complete circle tour of various sections of the area. Following are two of my favorite drives within the Telford–Crab Creek Tract.

MIDSECTION LOOP

This is a great one-day 110-mile tour through the midsection of the Telford–Crab Creek Tract. This trip can best be negotiated using the map "Channeled Scablands of Lincoln County," available for a small fee from the BLM Spokane office (see chapter 3).

Twin Lakes Recreation Area: From Davenport on US 2, drive 13 miles south on SR 28 to Harrington. Note the abrupt change from farmland to scabland as you travel south from Davenport. At Harrington, head west on Coffeepot Road to Highline Road to Twin Lakes Road, about 14 miles in all. Take Twin Lakes Road 2 miles to the Twin Lakes BLM Recreation Area and campground.

Coffeepot Lake Recreation Area: Return to Highline Road and Coffeepot Road, then head west on Coffeepot Road to the Coffeepot Lake turnoff to visit the lake.

Kolk lakes: Returning to Highline Road, follow it north, jogging west a few times to Hatten Road, and north to Swanson Schoolhouse Road, about 11 miles total. This leg of the trip takes you through scabland terrain and past several small *kolk* lakes, including Rock Lake, Wall Lake, Willow Lake, and Hatten Lake. At Swanson Schoolhouse Road, turn left and travel about 1 mile to Blenz Road. Turn right on Blenz and travel about 1 mile to Schuster Road. Follow Schuster west about 6 miles to SR 21, leaving the scabland for farmland in the process.

Govan Recreation Area: Turn right on SR 21 and travel north about 9 miles to Wilbur, on US 2. Then drive about 6 miles west to visit the Govan BLM parcel: take Govan Road south about 4.2 miles, then turn west on Lewis Bridge Road and follow it about 5 miles into the Wilson Creek scabland channel, over Lewis Bridge, and back west, then north to US 2 at Almira.

Telford Recreation Area: From Almira, head east again on US 2 about 19 miles to Creston. Stop to see the historical sign marking the capture of fugitive Harry Tracy (see sidebar). Continue east on US 2 about another 4 miles to the turnoffs on either side of the highway for the Telford BLM Recreation Area.

Take US 2 east 13 miles to return to Davenport.

ALMIRA TO ODESSA BACK ROADS LOOP

This driving tour takes you some 35 miles from Almira, on US 2, to Odessa, at the junction of SR 21 and SR 28, passing through creek channels not described earlier in this chapter. This trip can best be negotiated using the map "Channeled Scablands of Lincoln County," available for a small fee from the BLM Spokane office (see chapter 3). A 55-mile loop option brings you back to Almira via Wilbur.

Wilson Creek Channel: From Almira take US 2 about 0.5 mile east, then take Kiner Road south; you quickly enter some nice scabland flood channel bottoms before passing a small farm and crossing Wilson Creek about 3 miles south of the highway. Here, you can stop beside the road and enjoy the view both east and west into the large channel carved by floodwaters that likely entered and followed what was originally a much smaller waterway thousands of years ago. Like many scabland channels that appear way too large to have been created by the creeks and streams that flow through them today, the Wilson Creek channel is quite wide and deep at this point, illustrating nicely just how deep and swiftly flowing the ice-age floodwaters must have been when they passed through here many dozens of times.

Tracy's Cave: From here, Kiner Road climbs out of the Wilson Creek channel and passes through another few miles of scabland terrain before entering an elevated area of farmland. Out of sight over a ridge to the east is a small basalt grotto on private land called Tracy's Cave. It was named after Harry Tracy, the notorious killer and bank robber during the first decade of the twentieth century (see sidebar). Whether Tracy actually spent any time hiding in that cave—or atop Tracy Rock, for that matter, which is located in the nearby Telford Recreation Area—is unknown but open to debate and campfire storytelling.

Canniwai Creek Channel: From the point where you crossed Wilson Creek, continue south on Kiner Road about 11 miles to where the road jogs west for about 1 mile, then south again for another mile. Here, Kiner Road bisects Rimrock Road, where you turn east. For the next 4 miles, the road runs along the rim of the flood channel holding Canniwai Creek. Not quite so spectacular as the Wilson Creek flood channel, the Canniwai channel is nevertheless wide and rugged, a ragged basalt trough that carries the waters of Canniwai Creek south to join the Crab Creek channel some 10 miles or so to the southwest.

Reiser Falls: At a point slightly less than 4 miles from where you left Kiner Road and turned on to Rimrock Road, you will reach a spot where Canniwai Creek crosses under the road from the north. If you pull off to the side of the road and look down to your right where the creek emerges after having passed under the road, you can see a lively cascade of water called Reiser Falls. Note that in late summer months, the creek and falls will be merely a trickle, whereas in spring and early summer, you'll be more likely to see a nice little cataract of dancing and splashing water as it drops several feet.

Northern Loop option: Continuing east on Rimrock Road for another 3 miles, you arrive at SR 21, running north and south. If you take SR 21 north, you dip into the Canniwai Creek channel and cross the creek again in about 2.3 miles. The highway then rises into some higher terrain, crosses the small channel of Sinking Creek (don't you just love that name?), and in 21 miles from Rimrock Road joins US 2 near Wilbur. Head west on US 2 for 11 miles to return to Almira, for a total loop mileage of about 55 miles.

Southern route to Odessa: From the point where Rimrock Road joins SR 21, if you turn south you'll cross the channel called Marlin Hollow, then dip into and across the channel formed by Lake Creek, near Weaderspahn Lake.

Lakeview Ranch Recreation Area: You can take the Lakeview Ranch loop road, which leaves SR 21 at about 5 miles from where you departed Rimrock Road.

Odessa Craters: Taking this southern route on SR 21 also offers the opportunity to stop at the Odessa and Cache Crater Trails, about 7 miles south of the Rimrock Road turnoff.

About 13 miles from where you turned off Rimrock Road to SR 21, you'll reach Odessa in a one-way trip total of about 35 miles.

Grand and Moses Coulees

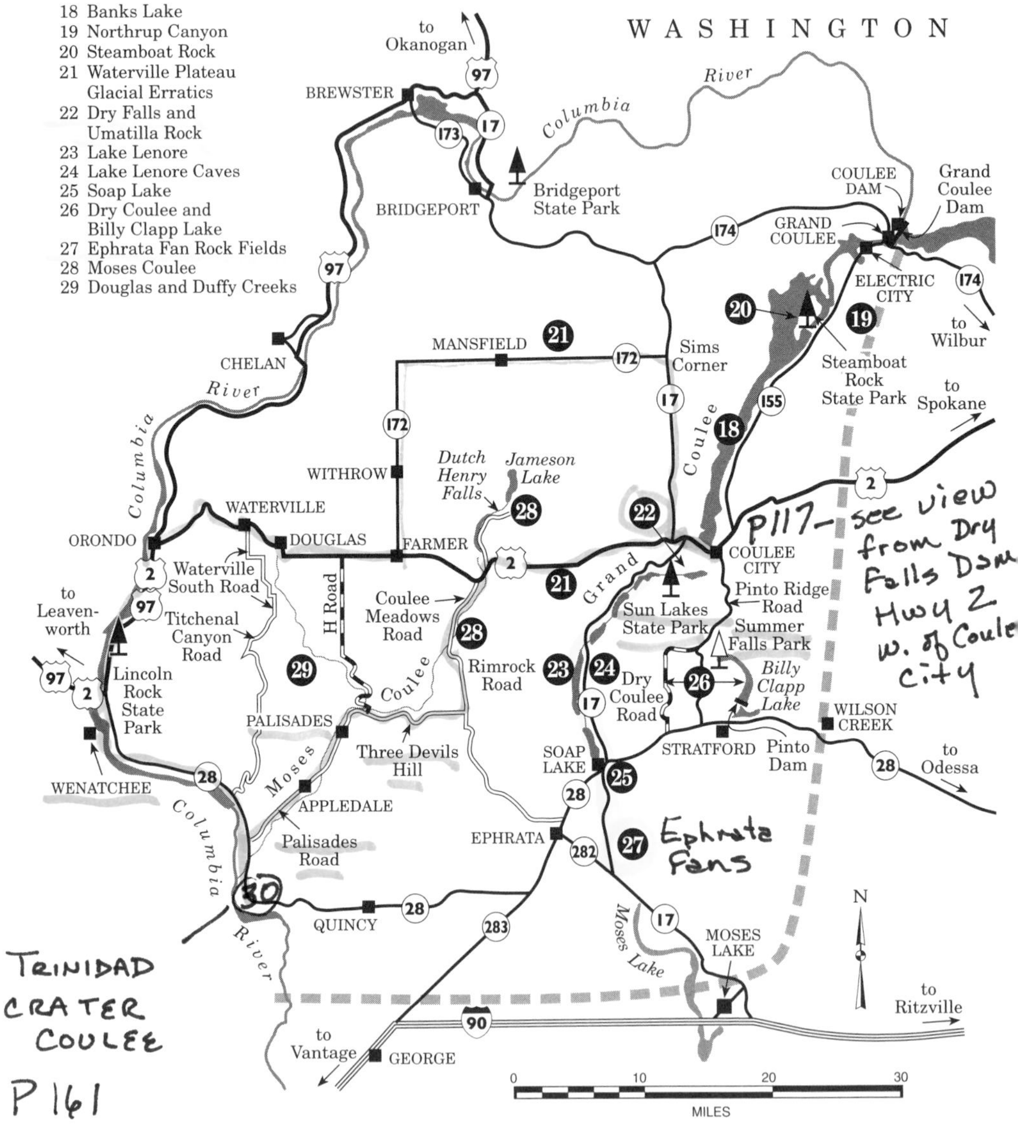
18 Banks Lake
19 Northrup Canyon
20 Steamboat Rock
21 Waterville Plateau Glacial Erratics
22 Dry Falls and Umatilla Rock
23 Lake Lenore
24 Lake Lenore Caves
25 Soap Lake
26 Dry Coulee and Billy Clapp Lake
27 Ephrata Fan Rock Fields
28 Moses Coulee
29 Douglas and Duffy Creeks
WASHINGTON
to Okanogan
97
BREWSTER
173
17
Columbia River
Bridgeport State Park
BRIDGEPORT
COULEE DAM
Grand Coulee Dam
174
GRAND COULEE
ELECTRIC CITY
174
to Wilbur
20
19
Steamboat Rock State Park
to Spokane
155
18
Coulee
MANSFIELD
21
172
Sims Corner
17
CHELAN
River
Columbia
172
WITHROW
Dutch Henry Falls
Jameson Lake
28
2
22
WATERVILLE
ORONDO
DOUGLAS
FARMER
COULEE CITY
2
21
Grand
Waterville South Road
H Road
Coulee Meadows Road
Sun Lakes State Park
Pinto Ridge Road
to Leaven-worth
97
Titchenal Canyon Road
28
Summer Falls Park
Lincoln Rock State Park
29
Rimrock Road
23
24
Dry Coulee Road
26
Billy Clapp Lake
97
2
Coulee
17
WILSON CREEK
PALISADES
STRATFORD
Pinto Dam
to Odessa
Three Devils Hill
SOAP LAKE
25
28
Moses
28
WENATCHEE
28
Columbia
APPLEDALE
EPHRATA
282
27
Palisades Road
30
QUINCY
28
283
17
N
Moses Lake
MOSES LAKE
River
to Ritzville
90
to Vantage
GEORGE
0
10
20
30
MILES
P117 – see view from Dry Falls Dam Hwy 2 w. of Coulee City
Ephrata Fans
TRINIDAD CRATER COULEE
P161

Pink Route = Wenatchee Map

Opposite page: *Deep Lake, below Dry Falls*

SIX

GRAND AND MOSES COULEES

I have always been fascinated by geographic features so large that they have their own ecosystems, their own species, their own weather patterns. I remember, as a boy, reading about the weather systems that could create megasnow- and windstorms around the upper two-thirds of Mount Shasta, simply because the mountain was so broad and so tall. Over the years I spent in and around Death Valley, I learned that the same was true in many ways within that unique and hostile region of the world. More than a dozen species of animals and insects, and more than three dozen plant species, are found nowhere else in the world but the Death Valley ecosystem.

Although the scablands' two largest coulees are part of a larger geographical region—the Columbia Plateau—Grand and Moses coulees are very similar in their stand-alone features that distinguish them from their surrounding terrain. This tract—basically two coulees with a combination of scabland and farmland in between—ranges from 40 to 50 miles wide and is about 60 miles long. It extends north and west to the Columbia, a bit beyond the actual scabland environment, but the ice-age features that are glacial rather than flood-related are interesting to see as well.

The magnificent, nearly 60-mile-long Grand Coulee is the key attraction of this westernmost tract of scabland, where floodwaters carved a gorge as deep as 1,300 feet in some places. The distance from the top of its towering basalt cliffs to the coulee floor below is so large, in fact, that differences in temperature from top to bottom can be 12 degrees Fahrenheit or more. Everything about Grand Coulee is huge. Within Grand Coulee are spectacular rock monoliths such as Steamboat Rock and the world's once largest waterfall, Dry Falls. Throughout the coulee, spectacular walls of basalt columns reveal the evidence of numerous lava flows in the separate layers or bands of columnar rock.

Throughout history, visitors to Grand Coulee have remarked about its beauty and sheer massiveness. In the 1880s, long before the flooding of upper Grand Coulee with Banks Lake, T. W. Symons traveled its length on horseback and commented, "We went north through the coulee, its perpendicular walls forming a vista like some old ruined roofless hall, down which we traveled hour after hour."

Dry Falls is the spectacular remnant of a waterfall found at the mid-point of Grand Coulee. The 3.5-mile-long scalloped precipice is some 400 feet high and ten times the width of Niagara Falls. The cataracts, when they were running, were thought to comprise the greatest known waterfall that ever existed. Geologists believe that water flowed in this vicinity at some 65 miles per hour through Upper Grand Coulee and over the rock face. So deep were the floodwaters, however, that had one been able to view the sight from above, the falls themselves would likely have looked like a mere dip in the swiftly flowing, 700-foot-deep torrent.

Now filled with lakes of various lengths and depths, the southern half of Grand Coulee terminates at a mineral lake—Soap Lake—and a bizarre sea of boulders that were flushed out through the coulee onto an outwash fan. Nearby are other coulees that formed when all the floodwaters could not pass through Grand Coulee and sought alternate routes. Dry Coulee and Trail Lake Coulee are two such places to explore. Billy Clapp Lake fills what used to be known as Spring Coulee. At one end is Summer Falls State Park, where a dramatic two-tiered waterfall flows only during irrigation season.

Just a short 15-mile drive to the west from Dry Falls is Moses Coulee, nearly as dramatic a sight as Grand Coulee, but devoid of reservoir water and a visitor center. The coulee was later named for Native American Chief Moses, but originally it was called *Sulk-stalk-scosum*, or "a place split from the sun." J Harlen Bretz believed that Moses Coulee had been carved by even more ancient floods or after a rerouting of the Columbia River by glacial ice. Most geologists now believe that the Okanogan Lobe of glacial ice blocked the natural route of the Columbia River and the river then discharged through Moses Coulee.

The best way to visit Grand Coulee is to plan spending an entire day, even a weekend, traveling from its north end to the south and taking in all the features contained within this monumental geologic feature.

AN UPSTREAM VIEW OF DRY FALLS

One of the most interesting views of the flood-ravaged landscape around Dry Falls can be seen from US 2 while crossing Dry Falls Dam at the south end of Banks Lake, just west of Coulee City. Four small finger lakes with the names Coulee, Lena, Table, and Junction lie close to the road and head in a southwest direction, as all well-behaved scabland *kolk* lakes do. The view to the south of the road that crosses the dam is of the approximately 1.5 miles of terrain that immediately precedes the sudden 400-foot drop over Dry Falls. You can't actually see the drop from this vantage point, but you can see the tall cliffs in the distance beyond it, and there is clearly a drop-off point on the southern horizon. The terrain here in that brief stretch of land before the big drop is scarred with notches and water-filled channels, potholes, and generally ragged basalt topography. This is private land not generally open to exploration, although the landowner has occasionally offered horseback riding tours of the terrain above the falls.

GEOLOGY OF GRAND COULEE

A brief look at how Grand Coulee was formed is important for understanding why it looks the way it does today. Before J Harlen Bretz came up with his theory regarding a giant ice-age flood, geologists had determined that Grand Coulee must have been formed when a giant section of ice called the Okanogan Glacial Lobe had traveled far enough south to block the Columbia River thousands of years ago and form what geologists call Glacial Lake Columbia. This lake spread out for nearly 100 miles to the east, inundating what is now the Spokane area and points farther east. When the great area of low-lying terrain that was occupied by this lake had been filled to capacity, its outflow was diverted south by the Okanogan Lobe of ice. This resulted in a diversion of the river to the south, forcing it to flow south at a point where Grand Coulee is today. When Bretz devised his flood theory, he conjectured that his "Spokane Flood" had caused Grand Coulee to form. It is now largely believed that it was a combination of both factors—the Glacial Lake Missoula floods and a rerouting of the Columbia River—that occurred during, and toward the end of, the last ice age.

The rerouting of the Columbia caused its waters to flow down Moses Coulee, which may have once been simply a gently sloped valley. When, over time, the Okanogan Glacial Lobe expanded in width while moving farther south, the waters of Glacial Lake Columbia were then diverted down through what is now Grand Coulee. Most geologists believe that the diversion of the Columbia River through Moses Coulee and Grand Coulee only served to establish the basic size and shape of the two coulees. As the flood-waters—first from Glacial Lake Columbia and later from the Glacial Lake Missoula floods—flowed into Grand Coulee (which would have been more of a valley then), this northern head of the coulee took in great volumes of water and widened out quite a bit, to as much as 6 miles in a few spots, until the water worked its way south and began to carve the deeper, narrower sections of Upper Grand Coulee.

In the middle of Grand Coulee's roughly 50-mile length, the walls of basalt that flank the great gorge decrease in height, and the terrain opens up for a few miles before Dry Falls signals a drop into a second section of deep canyon, Lower Grand Coulee. This phenomenon was caused by the presence of an anticline at the place where Upper Grand Coulee gives way to the lower coulee. An anticline is an arched, convex, upward fold in bedrock strata resulting from regional compression (to plain talkers—a hill). When floodwaters flowed over this anticline, the earth here was more resistant to erosion, so a deep gorge did not form at this point. When the more resistant strata had been passed, the waters continued their excavation of Lower Grand Coulee.

TOWNS OF THE GRAND AND MOSES COULEES AREA

- APPLEDALE is a tiny community in the lower part of Moses Coulee just north of SR 28. People have been growing apples here for more than 100 years. In 1909, the Great Northern Railway Company built a branch line from the Columbia River to Mansfield, and they named this spot Appledale because of the many apple orchards here. Only a handful of people live here now. There are no services.

- COULEE CITY is a Grant County town of about 600 people, situated at the junction of US 2 and SR 155, a site that was known as early as 1858 as the middle pass across the canyon. The location was for many years referred to as "McEntees Crossing of the Grand Coulee." Gone are the farms and grazing areas that once bordered the town to the north. This land is now under the waters of Banks Lake, which provides fishing, swimming, boating, and camping. Services include grocery stores, gas stations, restaurants, and motels.

- EPHRATA, on SR 28 between I-90 and US 2, is the seat of Grant County, with a population of nearly 7,000. Local lore says that a railroad worker thought the surrounding orchards and arid landscape were similar to the Holy Land and christened the area Ephrata, which is Hebrew for "fruitful." Ephrata was a convenient railway station, and as more settlers moved into Washington, the town was founded in 1901. Services include gas stations, small restaurants, and a motel or two.

- GRAND COULEE, population about 900, is located at the junction of SR 174 and SR 155, close to the 550-foot-high walls of America's largest concrete dam of the same name; the town serves as the area's supply point, with gas stations, grocery stores, restaurants, and shops for people who want to hike, bike, boat, or fish on Lake Roosevelt (the name for the Columbia River backed up behind Grand Coulee Dam). People come to Grand Coulee to shop and enjoy recreation activities, annual festivals, rodeos, the Laser Light Show, and the Toyland Winter Lighting.

- MANSFIELD is located north of Moses Coulee on SR 172. The population is slightly more than 300. The town was named after Mansfield, Ohio, by an early resident. Wheat growing sustained Mansfield for years, but a severe drought in the 1920s ruined the crops, and the town never really came back after that. Mansfield is known for two unusual activities among its citizens and others who come here: hang gliding and amateur rocketry. Go figure. Services include restaurants, a grocery store, and a gas station.

- PALISADES is an unincorporated community in Douglas County on the floor of Moses Coulee about 17 miles east of East Wenatchee. The backdrop of high basalt cliffs makes this a very scenic setting. A railroad used to pass through here but stopped using this route back in 1985. Palisades has a post office established in 1909 and a small elementary school, but little else remains here.

- SOAP LAKE, at the junction of SR 17 and SR 28, is a Grant County town on the shores of Soap Lake, with a population of about 1,700. The town's name came from the word *Smokiam*, a Native American word for "healing waters." Tribes used the lake's water to heal themselves and their animals for years before the area was settled by white pioneers. In 2002, the city announced preliminary plans to install the world's largest lava lamp (60 feet in height) as a tourist attraction. Services include gas stations, restaurants, and lodging.

- WATERVILLE, on US 2 just above the Columbia River across from Wenatchee, has a historic old town center. Services include gas stations, restaurants, grocery stores, and hotels.

PARKS AND CAMPING IN THE GRAND AND MOSES COULEES AREA

- BRIDGEPORT STATE PARK, off SR 17 just north of the town of Bridgeport, has camping, swimming, boating, and fishing.

- LINCOLN ROCK STATE PARK, on US 97 just north of Wenatchee, has camping, swimming, boating, and fishing.

- STEAMBOAT ROCK STATE PARK, off SR 155 south of Grand Coulee, has picnicking, camping, hiking, swimming, boating, and fishing.

- SUN LAKES STATE PARK, off SR 17 just south of US 2 at Dry Falls, has picnicking, camping, hiking, swimming, boating, and fishing.

BRETZ'S CLUES

As Bretz explored the scablands attempting to track the various pathways taken by floodwaters, he determined that one of the largest spillways to the Columbia had been Moses Coulee. Because Moses Coulee is located so far west of the other scabland areas, Bretz believed this deep flood channel might have originally been formed by a much earlier glacial melting from a different, more ancient ice age. Additionally, he theorized that Moses Coulee had been widened and deepened somewhat by his "Spokane Flood." Had Moses Coulee also acted as a strainer of the gravel and sand from the deposit-heavy floodwaters? Apparently so, for Bretz and his students found gravel deposits some 300 feet thick that started at the mouth of Moses Coulee and ran far upstream. The older, lower beds of this deposit were no doubt from earlier glacial streams, but the upper layers Bretz felt were certainly a result of the flood he was tracking.

18 BANKS LAKE

GETTING THERE: From US 2 at Coulee City, take SR 155 north, which follows the east shore of Banks Lake clear to the town of Grand Coulee at SR 174.

REGULATIONS: Discover Pass required for most access areas

Aside from Upper Grand Coulee's towering basalt cliffs and striking features such as Steamboat and Castle rocks, the most prominent feature is probably Banks Lake, named after Frank A. Banks, construction supervisor at Grand Coulee Dam. The 27-mile-long body of water filled the floor of the formerly dry coulee back in the 1950s when Dry Falls Dam was built and water was pumped out of nearby Lake Roosevelt to be stored here and used for agricultural purposes.

The nearly 25,000-acre lake averages 45 feet in depth and, at points, 3 miles wide; it is a true mixed-use reservoir. The northern and southern sections are designated as wildlife areas, with the chance to see a wide variety of birds, from shore varieties and waterfowl to birds of prey, such as bald eagles and peregrine falcons.

The rest of the lake is geared toward fishing, boating, and swimming. Put-in choices on Banks Lake include, from south to north, Coulee City Marina, Steamboat Rock State Park, a mid-length boat launch conveniently located adjacent to Paynes Gulch, and Sunbanks Resort in Osborne Bay at the north end of the lake. This is a large lake for small boats, but it offers that panoramic, small-fish-in-a-big-pond experience you can only get in a large body of water flanked by incredibly tall and scenic rock walls. Be aware

Banks Lake fills the floor of Upper Grand Coulee.

of larger, faster craft around you, as well as the occasionally stiff winds and choppy waters that move through here sometimes without advance notice.

Fishing in Banks Lake has long been regarded as a productive enterprise. Large walleyes are among the most prized catches, but anglers also descend upon Banks each fishing season to pursue rainbow trout, Kokanee salmon, catfish, and whitefish.

19 NORTHRUP CANYON

GETTING THERE: From Grand Coulee Dam at the junction of SR 174 and SR 155, drive south on SR 155 about 7 miles to mile marker 19. Go left up the Improved County Road for 0.5 mile and park at the Eagle View Site Lot.

REGULATIONS: State park fees may apply. Discover Pass required.

This side canyon takes off to the east in the northern part of Upper Grand Coulee. The canyon is now a Washington State Parks–operated nature sanctuary and popular hiking area. There is a good deal of history here that can only make your visit more enjoyable. Hikes through this canyon are best during fall, winter, and spring, before the hot weather and native rattlesnakes appear.

The Northrup Canyon area is a real mix of shrub-steppe and forestland vegetation.

Picturesque Northrup Canyon

Groves of quaking aspen and woods of ponderosa pine and Douglas fir are a sharp contrast to meadows of dry-land plants like sagebrush and bunchgrass. Photographers love this canyon for its wildflowers in spring, migrating songbirds, and a varied topography including green meadows, brown basalt cliffs, and forests of pine, fir, and aspen. Trout fishing is popular at Northrup Lake.

Bird-watchers frequent the canyon to see owls, hummingbirds, raptors, and other year-round feathered residents. In the winter months, bald eagles nest here and can mostly be seen along the south wall of the canyon. Other wildlife in the canyon includes mule deer and coyote.

Northrup Canyon Hike

Just a mile into the canyon, you'll begin to spot some amazing butte formations eroded into rugged shapes by the ice-age floods. Then the 3-mile round-trip trail leaves behind the flood-ravaged lower elevations and rises off into a scenic canyon area that really lets you feel as though you are off the beaten track. This was once a stagecoach route through flood-carved basalt cliffs. In the middle of the canyon, you'll come across the remains of an old homestead and an old wagon road that ran between Almira and Bridgeport. The road was used by stagecoaches and to haul freight wagons. A side road leads to a vacant house with outbuildings and an old homestead cabin, then heads up to Northrup Lake.

20 STEAMBOAT ROCK

Steamboat Rock appears to be a huge "island" of rock surrounded by the water of Banks Lake, but it is actually a peninsula, accessible by road from the lake's eastern shore. The basalt plateau resisted erosion from numerous Glacial Lake Missoula floods and was later nearly surrounded by water pumped in from Lake Roosevelt in the 1950s. The state park here has one of the best campgrounds in the state. A trail leads to the top of the rock where a wide plateau serves up some wonderful views of the coulee and Banks Lake below you.

Steamboat Rock Summit Hike

A 4-mile trail leads to the top of Steamboat Rock with grand views. After entering the park, follow signs to the trailhead area. From the parking area, the trail crosses the lower slopes, soon becoming very steep and rock strewn for a short stretch before entering into a notch through the cliffs. The trail soon splits, but either direction leads to the top. Take the left fork to see the western side of the summit plateau or the right fork to see the eastern side. Or explore both trails to get a more complete picture of Steamboat Rock's summit.

The trail to the summit at Steamboat Rock

21 WATERVILLE PLATEAU GLACIAL ERRATICS

GETTING THERE: On US 2 west of Coulee City, almost exactly 5 miles east of the Dry Falls Dam junction at SR 17, a gravel road leads a short way south of the highway to an erratic. Return east on US 2 about 3 miles and head north on SR 17 (less than 1.5 miles west of the Dry Falls Dam junction) about 12 miles to Sims Corner. From Sims Corner, head west on SR 172 about 8 miles to Yeager Rock, then through Mansfield; the highway

A number of large erratic rocks (that's erratic, not erotic!) are found throughout the Channeled Scablands; the ones mentioned so far in this book have all been rocks that were washed out of coulees by the ice-age floods or rafted to their current locations by floating icebergs. A number of erratics and other glacier-related features in and around the Waterville Plateau, though not flood features, were deposited at their current locations by glaciers. All of these are found north of the area where flooding occurred. But because you will be so close to these when you explore many of the scabland sites in this book, it makes sense to drive a bit farther and take a look at them.

takes a turn due south and passes through Withrow before rejoining US 2 at Farmer west of Moses Coulee.
REGULATIONS: Respect private property.

For example, you'll pass two or three large glacial erratics just off US 2 west of Coulee City. One of these (almost exactly 5 miles west of the junction of US 2 and SR 17) is on private land, but a gravel road leads up to it, and thousands of pictures have been taken of the rock, so you are probably safe to take a look if you stay out of the land-owner's fields.

Even more of these erratics and other glacial features can be found north of US 2, along SR 172 between Mansfield and Sims Corner, about 12 miles. Near Sims Corner are numerous erratics, as well as some eskers and kames, glacial features that are significant enough to have been noted as "the Sims Corner Eskers and Kames National Natural Landmark."

An esker is a long, winding ridge of sand and gravel deposited by a gla-cier, and often it is several miles in length. Due to their surprisingly uniform shape, eskers are sometimes confused with manmade structures such as rail-road embankments. A kame is another glacially created feature: an irregular mound made of sand, gravel, and till. These ingredients gather in a dip of depression atop a melting glacier and are then abandoned on the terrain at the point where the retreating glacier finally melts completely.

Heading west from Sims Corner on SR 172, you'll encounter Yeager Rock at about 8 miles. Frequently photographed, Yeager Rock is a 400-ton, two-story-tall erratic right on the very edge of the highway. Don't fall

A house-size glacial erratic northwest of Dry Falls

into the trap of marveling how the rock managed to stop just before rolling onto the road.

Other glacial erratics are found in and around towns in the area north of the scablands where glaciers covered the ground thousands of years ago. One way to find where some of these are is to ask townspeople in places like Mansfield, Withrow, Farmer, Douglas, and Waterville. Most erratics here are on privately owned farmland—respect landowners' property.

22 DRY FALLS AND UMATILLA ROCK

GETTING THERE: Dry Falls is on SR 17 between Soap Lake (at the junction of SR 17 and SR 28) and Coulee City on US 2. From Coulee City, head west of town on US 2 about 2 miles and turn south onto SR 17. The visitor center is slightly less than 2 miles down the road. To visit the features found at the bottom of the falls, drive just another mile or so south of the visitor center and take the turnoff to the left to Dry Falls–Sun Lakes State Park.

From Seattle via Ellensburg, drive east on I-90 and take exit 151 to

The first, and often the only, ice-age flood feature that many people have visited is Dry Falls, located smack dab in the transition zone between the Upper and Lower branches of Grand Coulee. Sitting just south of US 2 (a route frequently followed to Spokane from Wenatchee or points north of Seattle), Dry Falls is a much seen and often publicized geologic feature.

It was here that floodwaters from Glacial Lake Missoula rushed south through Grand Coulee and tumbled over what was once the world's largest waterfall. Geologists pretty much agree, however, that the surging waters here would have been rushing along some 200–300 feet above the rim of the falls, making the 400-foot drop somewhat less of a Niagara Falls on steroids and more (if one could have seen it from the air) like a wide

SR 283. Go north through Ephrata and continue on to Soap Lake. Turn north on SR 17, and continue 17 miles to the Sun Lakes State Park turnoff or about 18 miles to the Dry Falls Visitor Center. **REGULATIONS:** State park fees may apply. Discover Pass required at Sun Lakes State Park (below Dry Falls).

flow of muddy water with a dip in the spot where the receding cataract then stood.

Thousands of visitors routinely pull into the Dry Falls parking lot, walk to the edge of the drop-off to snap a picture, then get back in their cars and drive off. That's a shame, because the Dry Falls Visitor Center perching on the edge of the precipice is a well-equipped facility with a number of exhibits describing the geology of the falls, a book and gift store, a small auditorium for video presentations, and a marvelous set of picture windows overlooking the spectacular vista. The visitor center—a 1960s architectural statement if there ever was one—is set to be exchanged for a new facility sometime in the next decade; one hopes there will be similar views and a similar setting right at the edge of the precipice.

As one of the more developed and visited places within the Channeled Scablands, the Dry Falls overlook is flanked by fences and awash in warning signs. Nevertheless, it would still be quite easy to plummet off the 400-foot cliffs here if you were not careful or if you strayed out of the official tourist area. A fall would be not only fatal but extremely embarrassing, what with all the people at the nearby visitor center standing around taking pictures.

I should mention that I have always been intrigued by standing at the tops of things: cliffs, waterfalls, huge holes in the ground—all sorts of natural drop-offs. It always gives me the same sort of feeling you get at the top of that first, and highest, hill of a roller coaster: a growing sense of inevitability or realization that you are about to plummet to the bottom at any moment. One hopes you will not actually plummet over Dry Falls' basalt cliffs, but the feeling is definitely shared by many others I have spoken with.

If you'd like to put a bit more time into your visit here, make the effort to explore the floor of the great cascade at the bottom of the towering cliffs that once formed the rim of the falls. When you drive south beyond the visitor center, take the road that drops down to Sun Lakes State Park and

Dry Falls from the visitor center

resort area; the basalt cliffs begin to rise above you and before long, the visitor center is just a tiny white rectangle on the edge of the cliff high above.

Here at the bottom, after you have passed through a developed area of campgrounds, a golf course, and other amenities, a series of dirt roads wind around the base of the cliffs and take you to scenic pools including Perch and Dry Falls lakes. Rounding the southern end of Umatilla Rock—a massive basalt island at the bottom of the falls—is another amphitheater of Dry Falls, where Deep Lake lies.

Pick any one of these lakes, from Park Lake to Deep Lake, from Dry Falls Lake to Perch Lake. All of the lakes are small, but the fishing is good, and that always-looming dry waterfall towering above you will keep you checking over your shoulder for the first cascade of water over the edge. Some fun, huh?

Take Dry Falls Road north toward Dry Falls Lake and pull off to the side of the road, then head off on foot for awhile, keeping in mind that you are walking where the last tumultuous falls tumbled over the cliffs to your north before the end of the final Missoula flood. This is where the stupendous falls of Lower Grand Coulee at last ceased receding upstream, where they stopped carving out the canyon's deep, narrow channels of basalt after the flood waters had receded, or "walked backward" some 15 miles or more from the initial set of falls that formed near Soap Lake.

As you walk along the floor of the onetime plunge pool, now filled with eight or ten smaller remnants of that original plunge pool lake, you will come across bus-sized chunks of basalt, likely pieces of the cliffs to your north, pieces that eroded and broke away from the precipice of that cliff near the close of the last major flood event, some 15,000 years ago.

As is always the case when hiking the terrain around major flood features, you will feel very small strolling around the former plunge pool of that last great catastrophic flood that passed through here. The huge, scattered chunks of basalt tower above you as you wander among them. They seem quite solid and immoveable now, but they likely arrived at their current spots by rolling and bouncing along like pebbles below the surface of the floodwaters before coming to a stop where they rest today.

A word of warning: watch and listen for rattlesnakes if you are hiking around this area in the late spring or summer months.

Umatilla Rock Trail

The Umatilla Rock Trail located in Sun Lakes State Park consists of a 2.7-mile-long loop up to and around the top of the butte. The scenery is wonderfully bright and vivid here, the climate warm and arid with a definite Southwest flavor. The rock was named after the Umatilla tribe and language of the same name.

To reach the trailhead, drive down to Sun Lakes State Park and take the Dry Falls Road, which reaches a junction: you can turn left for Dry Falls Lake or turn right to Camp Delany (a private camp) and Deep Lake; take the left turn and follow the signs to Perch Lake, where you'll find a small trailhead on the left side of the road.

The trail to the top of the butte sometimes blends into the shrubby, craggy landscape, so you may lose it in spots. Sites to see on the floor beneath the falls include Perch Lake, Dry Falls Lake, Red Alkali Lake, Green Lake, Dry Falls from below, and, of course, Umatilla Rock. The 1,535-foot-tall butte towers like a giant fin in the middle of the Dry Falls plunge pool area.

Umatilla Rock was once an island in the midst of swirling waters during the great floods. Once you reach the top of Umatilla Rock, you'll find yourself standing 600 feet above the plunge pool beneath you.

23 LAKE LENORE

GETTING THERE: Lake Lenore is on SR 17 in Lower Grand Coulee, about 7 miles south of the Dry Falls Visitor Center and about 4.5 miles north of the town of Soap Lake.

Rather than containing one massive reservoir like Banks Lake in Upper Grand Coulee, the lower half of the coulee contains several smaller lakes, including the ones found at Dry Falls. Below these are Blue Lake, Lenore Lake, and Soap Lake.

Lenore Lake is about 4 miles long, with SR 17 running down the length of its east flank and its western border defined by basalt cliffs as high as 1,200 feet in some places. The intense summer heat between the walls of this deep gorge can be stifling.

Lake Lenore as seen from a cliffside cave

This is a nice quiet lake, since no motors are allowed. Although the cliffs along the east side of the lake make for few shore areas to hop out and explore, there are three such spots near the south end.

Fishing attracts most boaters here. Most anglers choose early morning or early evening to get out on this lake to avoid the heat of midday. Cutthroat trout are the prize pursued by most anglers three seasons of the year. The lake's famous Lahontan cutthroat trout were imported from Nevada, where residents (and the fish) know all about alkali lakes.

24 LAKE LENORE CAVES

GETTING THERE: Lake Lenore Caves are on SR 17 between Soap Lake (and the junction with SR 28) and US 2 at Coulee City. The caves are about 9 miles north of Soap Lake and about 7 miles south of Blue Lake. There are signs to help you, and the trailhead is just off the highway.
REGULATIONS: State park fees may apply.

The Lake Lenore Caves are a series of flood-carved openings where remnants of ancient campsites show that early humans used the caves for shelter, probably while traveling a nomadic route through the Inland Northwest. A short but fairly steep trail leads up and into the caves, which do not go back very far. The hike includes one steep staircase with steps that generally are coated with loose gravel. Climb these stairs with caution.

After viewing the caves, you can find other hiking opportunities if you pick your way up the cliff face, then up and over to another coulee running parallel to Grand Coulee. There are no real established trails here, so be careful not to get lost in the maze of basalt hummocks, washes, and thick brushy areas.

If you are making this trip during the summer months, beware of extreme heat, and also be aware that rattlesnakes, rubber boas, and bull snakes can all be found in this area. Be especially alert as you approach the cave entrances because, like humans, snakes like to cool off in the shade of the caves, especially during the heat of summer.

The trail to Lenore Caves

25 SOAP LAKE

GETTING THERE: Soap Lake sits at the junction of SR 28 and SR 17. From Coulee City on US 2, take SR 17 south through Lower Grand Coulee for about 17 miles. From Seattle via Ellensburg, take I-90 east to exit 151, then follow SR 283 and SR 28 north to Soap Lake.

At the southern end of Lower Grand Coulee sits Soap Lake—the lake and the town are named after it. Nestled beneath majestic basalt cliffs and rimrock slopes, the small lake has long been noted for its mineral-rich water and creamy black mud. Soap Lake is just over 2 miles long and less than 1 mile wide.

The first layer of Soap Lake is about 81 feet of mineral water; the second level is mudlike and consists of a stronger mineral with concentrations of unusual substances and microscopic life forms. The lake's two layers have not mixed in thousands of years. Scientists refer to lakes with this rare condition as meromictic, and only eleven such lakes are found in the United States.

At the turn of the twentieth century, Soap Lake was one of the most well-known mineral spas in the country. Before the development of sulfa drugs and penicillin, Soap Lake ranked with similar spas in Saratoga Springs, New York; White Sulfur, West Virginia; and Hot Springs, Arkansas—all of them well-known destinations for the treatment of illness and injury.

The name Soap Lake came from the word *Smokiam*, a Native American term for "healing waters." Tribes used the lake to heal themselves and their animals for many years before the area was settled by pioneers. In the early twentieth century, Soap Lake was a resort and health spa with four hotels and many rooming houses.

In the 1930s, the Veteran's Administration sent nine veterans to Soap Lake for treatment of Buerger's Disease. In November 1938, McKay Hospital was completed in the town of Soap Lake, and for many years the facility was used as a research center to study the therapeutic effect of the water. Today, visitors come for the mineral spas and bird-watching.

During spring and fall, the lake's large population of brine shrimp attracts numerous birds, including eared grebes, ruddy ducks, and many shore birds, even some marine species. Red-necked and Wilson's phalaropes and pectoral sandpipers arrive in mid-August and stay through September. In the fall, you can find northern shovelers, lesser scaups, and common goldeneyes.

Residents of Soap Lake, all 1,700 of them, have envisioned the town's revival by promoting it in a rather unusual way. Specifically, promoters are hoping to erect a 60-foot-tall functional lava lamp along the shores of Soap Lake, a goal they have pursued since 2002. Residents have even gone so far as to obtain the lamp itself, an advertising prop that was formerly used in Times Square, New York, by the Target Corporation, which donated it to

A northern shoveler is a common sight on Soap Lake (Photo © Alexandra MacKenzie).

Soap Lake in 2004. Unfortunately, the lamp still sits disassembled in storage as of 2012. Soap Lake city officials have yet to decide exactly how and where to display the unusual thematic object.

26 DRY COULEE AND BILLY CLAPP LAKE

GETTING THERE: To take a drive through Dry Coulee, from Soap Lake follow SR 28 east about 5 miles to Dry Coulee Road. Turn left (north) and follow the unimproved road through the lower half of the coulee about 8 miles until you reach Pinto Ridge Road. The paved road heads north (to Coulee City in another 8 or so miles) and south to rejoin SR 28 near the small town of Stratford. To see Summer Falls (remember that it only flows in the summer!), cross Pinto Ridge Road to stay on the gravel Dry Coulee Road and drive about 1.5 miles to a parking area at the north end of Billy Clapp Lake. To reach the south end of Billy Clapp Lake, return to Pinto

To the east of Lower Grand Coulee is some interesting scabland terrain where a few smaller coulees were formed by floodwaters pouring over the east wall of Upper Grand Coulee, then surging south. The floods carved two coulees here—Dry Coulee and Spring Coulee; the latter was dammed in 1947 and turned into a reservoir, Billy Clapp Lake. The ice-age flood feature Spring Coulee was referred to by J Harlen Bretz in 1932 as "a fine scabland canyon, with castle-like buttes, lateral subsidiary canyons, and cataracts notching its walls."

Dry Coulee is shaped like an 8-mile-long backward S with 200-foot basalt walls. A gravel road runs through the lower half of the coulee, passes through some scenic farmland, then connects with Pinto Ridge Road and the access road to Summer Falls, at the north end of Billy Clapp Lake.

Summer Falls is here only because of the Columbia Basin irrigation system. In the summer when irrigation water is flowing,

Ridge Road and take it south about 6 miles to SR 28 near Stratford, then another 2 miles east on SR 28 to County Road J NE (or, from Soap Lake, take SR 28 east a little more than 9 miles through Stratford to County Road J NE); take J NE north to the road's end, about 2.5 miles.

REGULATIONS: Discover Pass required at Summer Falls State Park and Billy Clapp Lake boat launch at south end of lake

the waterfall goes into action. During the fall and winter months, it simply dries up, sort of the opposite of a natural waterfall. The small state park at Summer Falls is a green oasis in the hot summer months, with picnic sites, a comfort station, and parking.

Billy Clapp Lake is a scenic 3-mile-long reservoir behind Pinto Dam. It was originally called Long Lake Reservoir but was later renamed for one of the originators of the Columbia Basin Irrigation Project. The geology of this place is ever present as you watch the lake waters lap against the lower walls of basalt cliffs that were carved by savage floodwaters thousands of years ago.

At the southern end of the lake, the Washington Department of Fish and Wildlife maintains a paved parking area with an outhouse, a courtesy boat dock, and two concrete boat ramps. The lake offers year-round fishing for yellow perch, crappie, rainbow trout, and walleye.

Storm clouds in Dry Coulee

27 EPHRATA FAN ROCK FIELDS

GETTING THERE: From the junction of SR 17 with SR 282, about 4 miles southeast of Ephrata, drive north on SR 17 about 1.5 miles to Trout Lake Road; the best place to see the large grouping of boulders is along this gravel road.

When I was a young boy, I collected rocks. Not in order to fill a glass case or box of mineral specimens—I simply liked to put them in my pockets whenever I was playing or exploring an area where multihued pebbles, sharp-edged rocks, and naturally polished stones were found in abundance and free for the taking.

On my return home, of course, my mother would generally command me to part with my blue jeans, which would have been grass stained, muddy, and perhaps even ripped after a day's hard work exploring. In so doing, she would also empty my pockets outside the back door and unceremoniously dump the contents of rocks on the ground. I didn't mind this because the gathering of the rocks had been my chief objective and the most fun.

In any case, it didn't take too many such rock gathering trips and pocket-emptying episodes for the ground outside our back door to become littered with rocks of all shapes and sizes. And when I first drove along some of the back roads that cross the Ephrata Bar, or Fan, as some call it, I was reminded

Flood-carried rocks of the Ephrata Fan

of these boyhood piles of rocks—only the ones I now found were magnified by a factor of a thousand or more.

The Ephrata Fan gets that name because—like an alluvial fan—it is an apron or fanlike area sloping downhill from a canyon (or, in this case, Grand Coulee) that is littered with debris that washed out of that same canyon over a period of decades and more of flood events.

Most geologists say that the Ephrata Fan is technically not an alluvial fan. Geologist David Alt, for example, who wrote *Glacial Lake Missoula and Its Humongous Floods,* says it should really be called the Ephrata Bar. Whatever you choose to call it, we are talking about a big field of debris covering more than 600 square miles that stretches from Ephrata and the mouth of Lower Grand Coulee south all the way to Moses Lake.

If you possess a vivid imagination, you can envision a giant pulling handfuls of rocks from his pockets and strewing them about the landscape just as I did while a boy. In this case, however, the rocks are boulders, some of them the size of cars and trucks. One, in fact, aptly named Monster Rock, is some 60 feet across. People like to climb to the top of the huge boulder of basalt and gaze around at all the other discarded rocks in all directions.

28 MOSES COULEE

GETTING THERE: To reach Jameson Lake from the west side of the state, take US 2 east from Waterville about 18 miles, to where the road drops into Moses Coulee. At this point, turn left (north) on Jameson Lake Road. From the east, take US 2 west from Coulee City and where the road drops down into Moses Coulee, turn right (north) on

Some call it Grand Coulee's poor relation. Others think it has nothing to do with the ice-age floods. But Moses Coulee, which experienced a geologic history very similar to Grand Coulee's, is a fascinating place to spend a day or a week. Only about 15 miles west of Grand Coulee, Moses Coulee seems somehow farther off the beaten track than that, as if it's 100 miles away from the scablands and their other geological features.

Jameson Lake Road. From either direction, take Jameson Lake Road north to reach Dutch Henry Falls in 3 miles and Jameson Lake in about 6 miles. The road continues north to Grimes Lake.

To tour the lower half of Moses Coulee, from US 2 near Jameson Lake Road, take Coulee Meadows Road south, where you'll encounter the McCartney Creek Meadow Preserve in about 4 miles. The road leaves the coulee here for about 4 miles, to reach an interesting little community called Rimrock Meadows, with tiny houses and cabins situated where the coulee walls and McCartney Creek are a scenic backdrop. At this point, Coulee Meadows Road becomes Rimrock Road. In the anticline section of Moses Coulee, the high basalt walls begin to lower and the land spreads out some between the upper and lower sections of the coulee. Just south of this community, take an abrupt right turn (west) on

Unlike Grand Coulee, Moses Coulee has no reservoir covering its floor. There are two small lakes way up in the north section of the coulee, but other than that, this is a dry coulee pretty much unchanged over the centuries. Like Grand Coulee, however, it has an upper and lower section, with an anticline in the middle, and the main road through the coulee descends the colorfully named Three Devils Hill and detours around much of the rugged midsections where, like Dry Falls, there are some dry cascades (though much smaller) and areas with an elevation drop from the upper half to the lower.

Other than the spectacular basalt walls that define the coulee itself, sights to see here include the huge hill of glacial till left from the Okanogan Lobe covering the upper part of the coulee thousands of years ago. As the lobe melted, the northernmost portion of Moses Coulee was left with clear evidence of the glacial ice that was once there.

At the north end of Moses Coulee are Jameson and Grimes lakes. Secluded, quiet, and mysterious are words that best describe Jameson Lake. The narrow width of this 1.5-mile-long lake makes it seem as though you are paddling down a river, not across a small lake. This popular fishing spot is a scenic *kolk* lake flanked by steep basalt cliffs and a real atmosphere of isolation and solitude. The quaint fishing resort and boat rental outlet called Jack's will take you back to lake resorts of the 1950s and '60s—quiet and family oriented. The small resort offers RV

Road 24 NW. This road continues west slightly less than 3 miles, then becomes an unpaved surface that winds about 4 miles down some steeply sloped switchbacks through a section of Moses Coulee called Three Devils Hill. Eventually this road turns into Palisades Road, which passes through Palisades in about 3 miles and Appledale in about 6 miles before joining SR 28 in about 5 miles at the southern end of Moses Coulee.

REGULATIONS: Discover Pass required in access areas

sites, two small cabins, four tent-only sites, a cozy little restaurant, and a country store. Dutch Henry Falls is found just off the main road through Moses Coulee south of Jameson Lake. A short hike takes you to a crevice in the canyon wall where the falls can be seen.

The Nature Conservancy has established the Moses Coulee Preserve near this same area. Even if you never liked the Beatles, you'll enjoy McCartney Creek Meadow. This area in the upper part of Moses Coulee had long been used to graze cattle and had become overgrown with nonnative plants. The Nature Conservancy purchased the land in the hopes of restoring the native vegetation and getting the regional community involved in the preservation and enhancement of the fragile shrub-steppe landscape. The 3,588-acre protected area provides habitat for a rich variety of birds, plants, and animals.

Much of the lower half of Moses Coulee is farmed, and two small communities, Palisades and Appledale, are located in this area. Palisades is pretty

Jameson Lake at the north end of Moses Coulee

much a ghost town, but it had a vibrant life for decades until trains stopped running through the coulee in 1985. Originally called Beulah Land, the small farming community was renamed 100 years ago for the steep basalt cliffs forming the walls of Moses Coulee.

29 DOUGLAS AND DUFFY CREEKS RECREATION AREA

GETTING THERE: From the north, approach the Douglas and Duffy Creeks Recreation Area via US 2 at Waterville. You can hike into the area from Moses Coulee at the south end, but the road is generally closed to vehicles due to flooding. To reach the Douglas Creek area, travel east of Waterville on US 2 for 8 miles, then turn south on H Road. Travel 7 miles down this gravel road into Douglas Creek Canyon. About 7 miles of road within the Douglas Creek watershed will take you to a variety of sites where you can park and explore. To reach the Duffy Creek area, from US 2 just west of Waterville, take Waterville South Road. After about 7 miles, turn west

Technically speaking, most of this recreation area is outside of the region referred to as Channeled Scablands. The lower reaches of this scenic canyon, however, were definitely swept over and reamed out by the ice-age floods. Also, this BLM-administered creek and canyon area, some 29,000 acres of it, empties into the lower half of Moses Coulee and should therefore be considered an offshoot or side canyon of the spectacular coulee.

An exploration of the Douglas and Duffy creek watersheds is a great way to inspect close up a transition zone from dry uplands or plateau land at about 2,000 feet in elevation to the flood-carved basalt formations found in the lower gorge, where it drops into Moses Coulee at about 1,000 feet in elevation. The major topographic features of this recreation area are the two descending watersheds, canyons, and riparian habitats of Duffy and Douglas creeks, one of which begins high on the eastern flank of Badger on Titchenal Canyon Road. Follow it for about 2 miles, turning left at the top of the hill where you will see a parking area and BLM signage indicating the entrance to the Duffy Creek area. Two other parking areas allow for deeper access to the Duffy Creek watershed: Rock Island Road (a 2-mile drive) or a BLM access road (about 3 miles long).

From the south on SR 28, turn north onto Palisades Road and follow it for about 10 miles. When the road turns east away from Douglas Creek, look for gravel Wagon Road, turn left onto it, and drive 1.5 miles. Park at one of the pullouts before the creek.

REGULATIONS: Dispersed camping

Mountain and the other on the southern edge of the Waterville Plateau.

The Douglas and Duffy creek watersheds formed a natural pathway for Native Americans who traveled to lower ground in the winter months. White settlers used the rugged thoroughfare as well. In order to transport lowland crops up to the Waterville Plateau and to points still farther north, the Great Northern Railway developed a line through Douglas Creek Canyon. This rugged route for a rail line demanded the construction of trestles, tunnels, and several steep grades. Most of these railroad remnants have long since deteriorated or been salvaged, but some stretches of this original grade can be found and hiked in this area.

Douglas and Duffy creeks are a beautiful part of the Moses Coulee uplands. Although it is a very isolated destination, the Douglas and Duffy creeks area regularly sees visitors interested in hiking, fishing, camping, and exploring the rugged but beautiful scenery of this rustic little corner of Douglas County.

Other attractions of this region include upland fields filled with wildflowers during the spring, numerous cliffs of basalt columns, and examples of unusual pillow basalt that formed when lava oozing forth from the earth came in contact with water. Hiking the lower part of the Douglas Creek Gorge as it drops spectacularly into Moses Coulee offers an outdoor geologic laboratory, not to mention a scenic wonderland of waterfalls, pools, and never-ending basalt rock formations.

The chance to observe native wildlife attracts many visitors to the Douglas and Duffy Creeks Recreation Area. A wide variety of birds make

Mule deer are frequently seen around Douglas and Duffy Creeks Recreation Area.

this rough and isolated terrain their home at least part of the year. These include loggerhead shrikes, prairie falcons, sage thrashers, and more than sixty species of migrating songbirds. Mammals spotted regularly in this area include coyote, mule deer, badgers, and white-tailed jackrabbits.

THE DRY FALLS REUNION

In 1994, the Washington State Parks and Recreation Commission honored the contributions of J Harlen Bretz by unveiling new exhibits and a plaque at the Dry Falls Visitors Center and scenic overlook. About fifty Bretz relatives gathered there on August 6 to view the unveiling of the plaque, which reads:

> Dedicated to
> **J Harlen Bretz**
> Who patiently taught us that
> catastrophic floods may sometimes
> play a role in nature's unfolding drama.
>
> "Ideas without precedent
> are generally looked upon
> with disfavor and men are shocked
> if their conceptions of
> an orderly world are challenged."
>
> —J Harlen Bretz, 1928
>
> 1994

GRAND AND MOSES COULEES AUTO TOURS

Exploring Grand Coulee by car is pretty much a matter of "Do I start at the north end and head south, or do I start at the southern end and head north?" After all, Grand Coulee is laid out roughly in one long north-south line. Whenever I have a choice, I usually prefer to explore most major scabland features by traveling in the direction taken by ancient floodwaters from Glacial Lake Missoula. It's not so much that I like going with the flow rather than fighting my way upstream; it's just that I think flood features make more sense when viewed geographically in the same direction they were originally created.

And so, in the case of large flood-carved channels like Grand Coulee, I think it makes the most sense to start at the north end, near the town of Grand Coulee. Your journey to reach the starting point is a bit convoluted if you're coming from the west side of the state, but I think it's worth your time to begin where the floodwaters first veered south and began to cut away this mammoth basalt trench, expressly designed by nature to efficiently transport water.

I also recommend reading the section at the beginning of this chapter regarding the formation of Grand Coulee, so you'll have the geology in your head before you set foot in this remarkable place.

Finally, a note about these suggested road trips through Grand Coulee: Though both tours can be combined and done in just one long day, if you want to explore each and every side trip, you're probably going to need a couple of days at a minimum. I have divided the Grand Coulee tour into two separate loops: the Upper Grand Coulee Loop, about 100 miles, which can be done in one day, and the Lower Grand Coulee Loop, about 83 miles, which can be done in a second day.

UPPER GRAND COULEE LOOP

To reach the northern extreme of the Grand Coulee from the Puget Sound area, take US 2 east to Wenatchee, then US 97 north to Brewster and cross the Columbia, then take SR 173 to Bridgeport and SR 174 to the town of Grand Coulee. From Spokane, take US 2 west to Wilbur, then SR 174 northwest to the town of Grand Coulee. At the town of Grand Coulee, begin your trip south on SR 155 through this monumental gash in the ground. Here at the northern end, you'll notice how wide the coulee is at this point, where floodwaters from the east would have been detoured south.

Banks Lake: As you drive down SR 155, the road hugs the eastern walls of the great gorge; to your right, the western wall and the widest part of Banks Lake is open to view. This section of Banks Lake has been designated as a protected wildlife area. High points along the east and west shores of the lake have been given colorful names and marked on maps. As you move south, look for Eagle Rock, Castle Rock, and Cache Butte, among others.

Northrup Canyon: After you have driven about 5 miles south of the town of Grand Coulee, you'll reach the turnoff for Northrup Canyon. Depending on how much time you have allowed, you may wish to turn off for the 0.5-mile drive to the parking area to visit (and perhaps hike in) this scenic and historic arm of the coulee. A Discover Pass is required to park in and visit Northrup Canyon.

Steamboat Rock: A little farther along, about 10 miles south of the town of Grand Coulee, you will see signs for Steamboat Rock State Park. A road, just a bit more than 3 miles long, takes off to the right for the scenic park with camping and picnicking, a boat launch, and a great hiking trail to the top of the huge basalt monolith. (Discover Pass required.)

Continuing south through the coulee, the distance between the basalt walls becomes narrower, with the west side higher than the east. Geologists think that spillovers from the floodwaters coursing through the Grand Coulee would have topped the eastern walls in several places, then flowed south to form flood features farther south such as Dry Coulee and Spring Coulee (now filled with the waters of Billy Clapp Lake). At the center of Grand Coulee's 50-mile length, the walls drop in height and the gap between them widens a bit. Here you leave the shore of Banks Lake and at about 25 miles from the town of Grand Coulee merge with westbound US 2, in another 2 miles passing the outskirts of Coulee City and Banks Lake Marina, then driving west about 1.5 miles across Dry Falls Dam.

Many people are confused by Banks Lake, thinking it is the reservoir created by Grand Coulee Dam. It is Dry Falls Dam, however, that keeps the water in Banks Lake. Grand Coulee Dam, north of the town of Grand Coulee, backs up the waters of the Columbia River to form Franklin D. Roosevelt Lake (commonly called Lake Roosevelt). Look over a map, and this confusion of dams and reservoirs around here will become much clearer. As you cross Dry Falls Dam, note the eroded scabland and fingerlike lakes to the south.

Waterville Plateau Glacial Erratics: If you have time, detour briefly west on US 2, where it crosses the southernmost reach of the Okanogan Glacial Lobe, which left a collection of glacially pushed rocks and debris now called the Winthrow Moraine. Look to your left along the first few miles of the highway here, and you'll spot some giant boulders that were pushed to their current location by glacial ice. After 5 miles, turn around and return east on US 2 about 3 miles and head north on SR 17.

In about 12 miles you'll reach Sims Corner, where you can explore "the Sims Corner Eskers and Kames National Natural Landmark." From Sims Corner, take another short detour west on SR 172 about 8 miles to Yeager Rock. You've now visited the three easternmost examples of these glacial erratics, so return east on SR 172 to Sims Corner, then turn left to continue north on SR 17 about 7 miles to SR 174. Turn right (east) on SR 174 to return in about 20 miles to the town of Grand Coulee and complete your 100-mile loop.

LOWER GRAND COULEE LOOP

[handwritten: 83-mile loop Coulee City- Ephrata fans]

To maintain the north-south orientation of these journeys in the Channeled Scablands, begin this loop on US 2 at Coulee City, at the east end of Dry Falls Dam. Head west on the highway and when you have crossed the dam, turn left (south) onto SR 17 and head down into Lower Grand Coulee.

Dry Falls and Umatilla Rock: On SR 17 in Lower Grand Coulee, you soon begin seeing the ragged buttes and cliffs of Dry Falls, and in 2 miles from the dam you'll reach the turnoff for the Dry Falls Visitor Center and viewpoint. Stop here and take a look down at the Dry Falls panorama, as well as the interesting displays at the visitor center. Travel south on SR 17 another 1.5 miles, and if you have time, take a short detour down into Sun Lakes State Park, where you can drive or hike along the bottom of the huge plunge pool area below Dry Falls. The trail to Umatilla Rock is found here too. (Discover Pass required in Sun Lakes State Park.)

Lake Lenore; Lake Lenore Caves: Continuing south on SR 17, you enter the Narrows section of Lower Grand Coulee, along the shore of Lake Lenore. At a point about 14 miles from the Dry Falls Visitor Center, you'll see the turnoff for Lake Lenore Caves. If you have the time, hike up the steep but fairly short trail into the flood-carved openings to see shelters used by early Native Americans thousands of years ago.

Soap Lake: Continuing to drive past Lake Lenore in Lower Grand Coulee, you are now nearing the southern end of Grand Coulee and in about 9 miles from the caves you'll reach Soap Lake—both the lake and the town of the same name. If you have more time for exploring, take a short detour south.

Ephrata Fan Rock Fields: Continue south through Soap Lake on SR 17 past the junction with SR 28 and in about 9 miles from that junction, turn left on Trout Lake Road. Immediately you will begin to see a large collection of erratic rocks, some basalt and some granite, all of which floated, tumbled, and otherwise arrived here during the great floods through Grand Coulee. Look for the largest of these rocks on the left side of the road, fittingly called "Monster Rock." If you have the time, take a short hike out around these scattered boulders in this strange, almost lunar landscape. After your explorations, return north 9 miles on SR 17 to the junction with SR 28 just south of Soap Lake.

Dry Coulee and Billy Clapp Lake: Head east on SR 28; if you have time for a brief detour to Billy Clapp Lake, drive about 9 miles east to county road J NE, then turn north to reach the lake in about 2.5 miles. Return to SR 28 and head west about 4 miles to Dry Coulee Road; turn right (north) and follow the unimproved road through the lower half of the coulee for about 8 miles until you reach Pinto Ridge Road. If it's summer and you want a quick side trip to see Summer Falls (it only flows in summer), cross Pinto Ridge Road to stay on gravel Dry Coulee Road for about 1.5 miles to a parking area at the north end of Billy Clapp Lake. After your visit to the falls, return to the junction with paved Pinto Ridge Road and turn right (north) to return to Coulee City in another 8 or so miles, completing your 83-mile loop. (Discover Pass required at Summer Falls State Park.)

MOSES COULEE

This 45-mile drive through Moses Coulee lets you experience glacial advances of ice, the great floods at the close of the last ice age, and some more current history in the form of stagecoaches, railroads, and early agricultural efforts here.

From the west side of the state, take US 2 east to Wenatchee and continue north on US 2 to Orondo, about 13 miles north of Wenatchee. Continue east on US 2 through Waterville and all the way to where the highway drops into Moses Coulee—about 27 miles from Orondo. When you have dropped into the coulee floor, US 2 turns left (north). About 2 miles farther, at a point where US 2 turns east again, leave the highway and head north on Jameson Lake Road.

From the east side of the state, take US 2 west to where it drops into Moses Coulee, about 17 miles west of Coulee City. Turn right (north) on Jameson Lake Road.

Jameson Lake: Head north on Jameson Lake Road into the uppermost part of Moses Coulee. As you travel north, note the massive rounded hills of rocks and gravel to your right. This is glacial till left behind after the last finger from the Okanogan Glacial Lobe pushed its load of gravel and rocks and left it here at this point in Moses Coulee before retreating and melting away at the end of the last ice age. In about 6 miles north is Jameson Lake, a popular fishing spot and scenic *kolk* lake flanked by steep basalt cliffs and a real atmosphere of isolation and solitude.

Dutch Henry Falls: Returning the way you came, note the deep gash in the cliff wall on the right (west) side of the coulee wall about 3 miles south of Jameson Lake. This is the mouth of Dutch Henry Draw, a side canyon that carries small volumes of water in a creek that tumbles down into Moses Coulee from the eastern slope of the Waterville Plateau, which is about 6 miles to the west. Dutch Henry Falls can be reached by stopping your car opposite the notch and hiking a short trail to a shadowy green space with a waterfall and small pool inside the walls of this crevice.

McCartney Creek Meadows: Heading south down the coulee, rejoin US 2 and follow it west a mile or so until the spot where it heads out of the coulee to the west, then turn left onto Coulee Meadows Road and continue south about 4 miles to the McCartney Creek access road.

Rimrock Meadows: After exploring the McCartney Creek area, continue south on Coulee Meadows Road. The southern tracking road leaves the coulee here for about 4 miles to encounter an interesting little community called Rimrock Meadows, with tiny houses and cabins situated where the coulee walls and McCartney Creek are a scenic backdrop. This is the anticline section of Moses Coulee, where the high basalt walls begin to lower and the land spreads out some between the upper and lower sections of the coulee. After this community, you take an abrupt right turn (west) on Road 24 NW.

Three Devils Hill: This road continues west slightly less than 3 miles, then its paved surface ends as it winds about 4 miles down some steeply sloped switchbacks through a section of Moses Coulee called Three Devils Hill. The road now passes through a scenic, steeply dropping terrain with Rattlesnake Creek running down below you on the right. This is roughly the equivalent of the Dry Falls area of Grand Coulee, with an elevation drop of a few hundred feet but no dramatic dry falls. As you near the bottom of the Three Devils area, you get some great views of Lower Moses Coulee, with its 900-foot basalt cliffs and rich farmland, green with the waving stalks of corn in the summer months.

Douglas and Duffy Creeks Recreation Area: Across the coulee to the right, you will see the canyon that Douglas Creek winds through before it enters Moses Coulee. Douglas Creek then takes in the waters of Rattlesnake Creek before heading southwest to join the Columbia at the mouth of Moses Coulee. To the south of this region is a rugged, hilly area administered by the BLM that offers a number of hiking trails and access to some scenic canyon and plateau country. You must reach this parcel of recreation land from the east just before dropping into the Three Devils area, or from the south via Lynch Coulee and Baird Springs Road, then up Overen Road. Finding this area is a bit tricky, and contacting the BLM office in Wenatchee is the best way to get good directions to its Moses Coulee tracts and a helpful map (see chapter 3).

Palisades: As the road through Moses Coulee takes a sharp turn to the left (southwest), you enter the historic Palisades area of the coulee. The road, now called Palisades Road, passes through some lovely farmland on the floor of the coulee. It reaches Palisades in about 3 miles and Appledale in about 6 miles before dropping in about 5 miles to SR 28 at the mouth of Moses Coulee, which joins with the Columbia River. Note the large flood bar here at the mouth, a remnant of the ice-age floods thousands of years ago. From here, you can take SR 28 either west, to return north to US 2 at Wenatchee, or east, to Quincy, Ephrata, and Soap Lake or other points east.

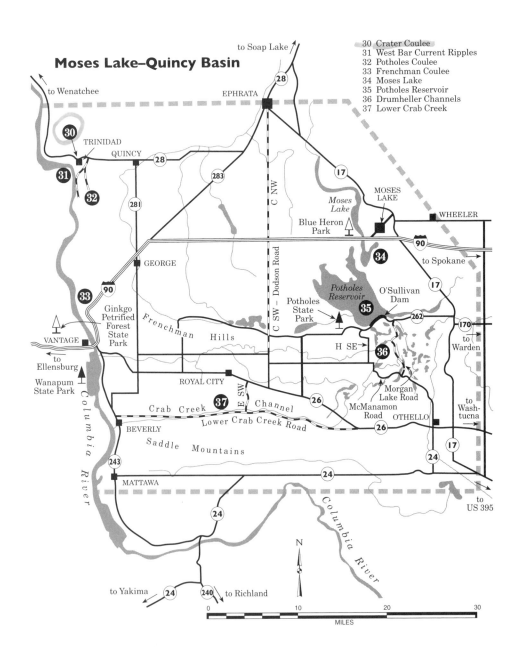

Moses Lake–Quincy Basin

30 Crater Coulee
31 West Bar Current Ripples
32 Potholes Coulee
33 Frenchman Coulee
34 Moses Lake
35 Potholes Reservoir
36 Drumheller Channels
37 Lower Crab Creek

to Soap Lake
to Wenatchee
EPHRATA
TRINIDAD
QUINCY
MOSES LAKE
WHEELER
Moses Lake
Blue Heron Park
to Spokane
GEORGE
Potholes Reservoir
O'Sullivan Dam
Ginkgo Petrified Forest State Park
VANTAGE
to Ellensburg
Wanapum State Park
Frenchman Hills
Potholes State Park
H SE
to Warden
ROYAL CITY
Crab Creek
Channel
E SW
Morgan Lake Road
McManamon Road
OTHELLO
to Washtucna
BEVERLY
Lower Crab Creek Road
Saddle Mountains
Columbia River
MATTAWA
to US 395
Columbia River
to Yakima
to Richland
N

0   10   20   30
MILES

C NW
C SW – Dodson Road

Opposite page: *The vista above Potholes Coulee*

SEVEN

MOSES LAKE–QUINCY BASIN

South of Grand Coulee and west of the Telford–Crab Creek Tract of scablands lies the shallow, bowl-like depression called the Quincy Basin. This tract of scabland and gravel beds ranges from 25 to 30 miles wide and is about 20 to 25 miles long, covering roughly 600 square miles.

Into this region, floodwaters gushed from Grand Coulee and surged out of the Telford–Crab Creek area. Here the water collected and filled the basin until it found three low points to the west and one to the south: The three westerly egress points were Crater Coulee to the north, Potholes Coulee in the center, and Frenchman Coulee in the southwest corner of the basin. The southern exit route was through Drumheller Channels.

The first egress point, Crater Coulee, is now chiefly a place to look at the view. Potholes Coulee offers great hiking, camping, and fishing, plus magnificent vistas of the dry, multitiered waterfalls left after floodwaters thundered over cliffs to join the Columbia River. Frenchman Coulee is a horseshoe-shaped recessional coulee with incredible views from above. There is plenty of hiking here, a boat ramp to the Columbia, and even a place for rock climbers to test their skills at the Feathers, a long row of basalt columns standing on end in the center of the basalt amphitheater.

To the south in the Quincy Basin is the dramatically eroded corridor known as the Drumheller Channels. This mazelike region of buttes and small canyons represents the fourth exit point for floodwaters gathering in the Quincy Basin. Today, it is also home to Columbia National Wildlife Refuge and is the site of the annual Sandhill Crane Festival.

Also left from the passage of water through the Quincy Basin are huge gravel bars, oversize flood ripples, and the scenic corridor through which Crab Creek makes its way west to the Columbia River. The longest creek in the Channeled Scablands, Crab Creek begins not far from Reardan and flows into the Columbia near Beverly. The Lower Crab Creek corridor is nestled between the Frenchman Hills, the site of some flood-rafted erratics off SR 262, and the Saddle Mountains.

Sentinel Gap was cut through the Saddle Mountains by the ancient Columbia River. With each Glacial Lake Missoula flood, waters rushed south from other scabland tracts and had other routes by which to reach the Columbia River. As a result, Sentinel Gap did not experience the same phenomenal force of the entire flood as did Wallula Gap (see chapter 8), so Sentinel Gap didn't cause a major backup of water the way Wallula Gap did.

....

THE SOUND OF SILENCE

In the Drumheller Channels, perhaps more so than at any other place I have visited in the Channeled Scablands, there exists a silence and sense of isolation I don't think I have experienced anywhere other than the saline floor of Death Valley. People may think they know what silence "sounds" like, but I'm convinced the majority have experienced these silent episodes in populated areas, where the quiet can be judged only in juxtaposition to the normal urban sounds that prevail. The silence of a city street at night, the quiet of an empty office building when you are the only worker still at your desk, the solitude of an empty sports stadium when you are the sole spectator sitting in the stands . . . These are the sorts of experiences people cite when you ask them to describe the quietest place they have ever been.

But just as the darkness of a bedroom with the lights turned off can never compare to the blackness of a cave with your lantern switched off, so is urban silence less pure, less absolute than the silence of natural settings. If we listen hard enough, even in the most noiseless of urban settings, there will always be the murmurs of man all about us—the humming and whirring and buzzing of noises we don't even realize are constantly in our ears until we withdraw from that urban setting and experience a truly natural environment far from the influence of man.

Out in these places away from the domain of the human race, far from the machines, the music, from television and traffic and talk, you can slowly begin to understand what the true silence of the natural world is all about. This is the time when the sounds associated with civilization will slowly fade farther and farther away.

"Speech is civilization itself," wrote Thomas Mann in 1924 in *The Magic Mountain*. "The word, even the most contradictory word, preserves contact—it is silence which isolates."

But it is this same isolation from civilization, from contact with other humans, that allows for a contact to be made with nature and oneself. More to the point, it is that isolation and silence that allow a person to make contact with the dimension of time, the ruler of this and all other land-scapes formed by geologic events occurring over numberless millennia.

In this natural world of silence, a person is best able to begin imagin-ing the sounds that must have accompanied the natural forces that cre-ated this place. It is a silence that also allows you to imagine what people who may have lived here 15,000 years ago—and there is a very good possibility that people were here—might have heard and felt and seen through terrified eyes as a series of great, brown, thundering waves of slurry flowed across a formerly green and rolling landscape, first tearing at the soil, then snatching at the basalt columns beneath, peeling them off the cliff faces like some hungry grizzly peeling bark from a yellow pine.

At first, there would have been that same silence a visitor to this place experiences today. Then, even before the water arrived—perhaps as much as a half hour before—there would have been a thunderous noise, a strong wind, perhaps even the sense that there was the mist of some unseen moisture source in the air. Then the ground would have begun to shake and the hunters and gatherers experiencing all this might have received their first sensations that something quite ominous was about to occur.

The sounds of silence in this great geological landmark enhance the already powerful sensation it gives off as being a wilderness area worthy of both respect and caution.

GEOLOGY OF THE DRUMHELLER CHANNELS

The Drumheller Channels are, to put it mildly, the epitome of geologic chaos. Although the Channeled Scablands as a larger region are already an unruly collection of geologic landscapes with diverse and dramatic features, the Drumheller Channels are an especially ragged, jumbled, utterly undisci-plined landscape, even given the circumstances of their creation.

Even geologist J Harlen Bretz, who first proposed the theory of a great flood, was impressed with the Drumheller Channels' braided configura-tion. The typical branch pattern of most rivers involves numerous small tributaries joining larger ones and these eventually connecting with one master river. The profile appears much like a tree, with tiny twigs leading to small branches, then bigger ones, then the trunk of the tree. Braided streams, on the other hand, can run side by side, join together, crisscross one another, and in other ways look nothing like the typical channels of most streams and rivers.

Geologists now consider the Drumheller Channels to be the most spectacularly eroded area of its size in the entire world.

The look of the Drumheller Channels is clearly unique, even by scabland standards. There is no single deep coulee through which the bulk of flood-waters flowed. Nor were any major waterfalls left behind, as in so many other scabland locations. Instead, there is a veritable maze of channels that start and stop, intersect, twist, and turn on their way generally south. When Bretz explored and mapped this region, he counted 150 individual channels and more than 180 rock basins or potholes carved by the floods.

The Drumheller Channels tract is named after the Drumheller family stock ranch, which operated in the area at the time of Bretz's first visits here. It consists of a 50-square-mile area east of the Frenchman Hills and south of Quincy Basin. During Pleistocene flood events, Quincy Basin filled with water that flowed into it from the north and east. The pressure of all this water in the basin caused three major cracks to open along its western boundary and allowed water to escape and flow through Crater Coulee, Potholes Coulee, and Frenchman Creek Coulee into the Columbia River. The huge dry falls and deep channels that remain at these three locations reveal the path of untold millions of gallons of water, but they did not by any means represent the greatest exit path from Quincy Basin.

That route was through the Drumheller Channels, which acted as a sort of chute through which a broad cascade some 8 to 12 miles wide flowed at speeds estimated at some 65 miles an hour. An elevation drop of 150 feet or more helped accelerate the speed of the water as it passed through here.

It seems clear that velocity was not the only factor involved in the shaping of this region's unique landscape, however. A twisting, churning, whirlpool-like performance of the water was likely the result as cascades arrived here from the west, north, and east, all converging to pass through the narrow trough. The east end of the Frenchman Hills represents a barrier that flood-waters would have pummeled with tremendous force, causing a rebound of sorts and adding to the potential for swirling or whirlpool effects.

There may also have been an effect on the flow of water through the Drumheller area as floodwaters departed the channels and split in two. Half the flow turned west after passing through the Drumheller Channels and inundated lower Crab Creek as it made its way west to the Columbia through a deep channel between the Frenchman Hills and the Saddle Mountains. The rest flowed south toward what is now known as the Pasco Basin but at the time was a body of water that geologists refer to as Lake Lewis (see chapter 8). This 2,000-square-mile lake was backed up behind the narrow exit called Wallula Gap. So restrictive was this narrow passageway that Bretz soon realized during his field studies that the huge lake behind Wallula Gap would have backed water up the Snake River, up into Washtucna Coulee, and probably as far north as the location of the Drumheller Channels. This could mean that rising water might have enhanced the underwater churning and cutting of the channels, accentuating the phenomenal erosional activity there.

TOWNS IN AND AROUND MOSES LAKE–QUINCY BASIN

- BEVERLY, a small town located just south of the junction of SR 243 and Lower Crab Creek Road where Crab Creek flows into the Columbia River, has a few hundred residents and is just a few miles downriver from Wanapum Dam. Beverly played host to hundreds of railroad workers from 1905 to the early 1920s when the Milwaukee Railroad was being built. In 1977 the Milwaukee filed bankruptcy, and by the early 1980s the state had removed the rail line from Beverly to a junction near Royal City. This tiny town has virtually no services for visitors.

- GEORGE, Washington, is located on I-90 south of Quincy, at the western edge of the Columbia Plateau before it begins its descent to the Columbia. It is an agricultural hub. Services include gas stations and a restaurant named the Martha Inn.

- MOSES LAKE, on I-90 at its junction with SR 17, began in 1910 as a supply town for farmers and ranchers. The town was called Neppel, after one of the settlers' hometown in Germany. In 1938 US 10, a former transcontinental highway, was built through the town. That same year, residents voted to change the town's name to Moses Lake. In the early 1940s, the US Army established a bomber training base, later to become Larson Air Force Base. By 2001 the city's population had neared 16,000. Today, all services can be found here, from gas stations to restaurants to motels.

- OTHELLO's first settlers were Ben and Sam Hutchinson, who built a cabin along Crab Creek in 1884. Other homesteaders followed, and a town was formed in 1907 when the Chicago, Milwaukee, and St. Paul Railroad ran a track through the area; the highway paralleling those tracks is now SR 26. In the early 1950s, the Columbia Basin Project brought irrigation to the Othello area, increasing both agriculture and commerce. The town of 5,800 people has been home to the Sandhill Crane Festival since 1998. Services include hotels, restaurants, grocery stores, and gas stations.

- QUINCY, on SR 28 at its junction with SR 281, is a town in Grant County with about 5,000 people. Quincy was founded as a railroad camp during construction of the Great Northern Railway in 1892 and was officially incorporated on March 27, 1907. It was named after Quincy, Illinois. Concerts at the nearby Gorge Amphitheatre bring a variety of people through the town in the summer months. Services include hotels, restaurants, grocery stores, and gas stations.

- ROYAL CITY, on SR 26 between Othello and Vantage, was founded in 1956. The small farming community (population 1,800) is most well known for growing a wide variety of crops, including apples, cherries, peaches, hay, melons, potatoes, onions, wine grapes, pears, and corn. The pleasant climate most of the year makes the area popular with birders, hunters, and golfers. Services include restaurants, a gas station, and grocery stores.

- VANTAGE is located on the west side of the I-90 bridge crossing the Columbia just north of Sentinel Gap. Vantage is home to fewer than 100 people, and the town is best known for Ginkgo Petrified Forest State Park, home to one of the most unusual fossil forests in the world—and its visitor center has a fine exhibit on the ice-age floods (see "An Introduction to the Ice-Age

Floods" in chapter 1). Services include a gas station and a restaurant that's occasionally open.

PARKS AND CAMPING IN AND AROUND MOSES LAKE–QUINCY BASIN

- BLUE HERON PARK, just off I-90 at the west edge of the town of Moses Lake, has picnicking, swimming, and fishing.

- GINKGO PETRIFIED FOREST STATE PARK, just north of I-90 at Vantage, has swimming, boating, and fishing.

- POTHOLES STATE PARK, off SR 262 at the west end of O'Sullivan Dam, has camping, swimming, boating, and fishing.

- WANAPUM STATE PARK, off SR 243 between SR 26 and Beverly, offers camping, hiking, and boating.

This slot canyon was created by floodwaters through Crater Coulee.

30 CRATER COULEE

GETTING THERE: Crater Coulee can first be viewed from SR 28 at a point some 3 miles west of Quincy as you head toward the Columbia River. Continuing west along SR 28, you can see the coulee deepening until it drops some 300 feet into Lynch Coulee, which approaches the Columbia River from the north. The dramatic drop of the highway as it descends to the Columbia reflects the equally significant descent of ancient floodwaters.

When J Harlen Bretz determined in the early 1920s that there had been three western exit paths for floodwaters that inundated Quincy Basin, he declared that the northernmost of these had been Crater Coulee. Crater Coulee is not a full-scale recessional waterfall with well-defined cataracts and erosion-carved alcoves, such as the other two prominent exit points for Quincy Basin (Potholes Coulee and Frenchman Coulee). The reason is that the terrain here was slightly higher (by almost 80 feet) than the other two exit points. This meant that not every flood from Glacial Lake Missoula would have come through here, so less erosion took place overall. Only the biggest floods would have provided enough water to spill over the lip of Crater Coulee. Crater Coulee was clearly a pathway for ice-age floodwaters as they departed Quincy Basin and plummeted into the Columbia, carving away the terrain as they flowed.

31 WEST BAR CURRENT RIPPLES

GETTING THERE: From Wenatchee take SR 28 east to where it climbs the hill up Babcock Bench above

As you descend SR 28 alongside Crater Coulee, you pass the small community of Trinidad, perched above the resort and subdivision of Crescent Bar. Here a small collection of homes and a few commercial businesses hunker down atop the small the Columbia River heading toward Quincy. As you climb the hill, West Bar and its current ripples are visible to your right and below, across the Columbia River on the west side. From Quincy, follow SR 28 west down the hill toward the river. From either direction, the best way to see West Bar is to pull off on the right side of the road where a good view of the river to the south is available. Or you can take Crescent Bar Road and stop along the shoulder where it's safe to look down at West Bar and its current ripples. Before you reach the top of the climb up the hill above Crescent Bar on SR 28, you'll see a store and gas station on your right; turn in here and park by the store, then walk to the back of the parking area to look down into the slot canyon that captured some of the water from Crater Coulee and directed it down to where the luxury homes of Crescent Bar now stand.

bench of land at the halfway point of the highway's descent to the river. After you head down to the river, take a few moments to pull into the parking lot of the gas station—convenience store and walk to the back of the lot, where you can gaze down at a deep slot canyon carved by floods through Crater Coulee and direct your eyes to the homes of Crescent Bar below.

At this point, you can continue all the way down to the Columbia River via SR 28, which then heads north to Wenatchee, or you can take a turnoff south to Crescent Bar Road, which dead-ends at the Crescent Bar resort and housing subdivision. Either way, turnouts allow you to view the phenomenal current ripples of West Bar, which extends along the west shore of the Columbia River where it makes its big bend here.

The first view I had of West Bar was through a telescope in the backyard of friends who live in a cliff-side home overlooking the Columbia at Trinidad. Many scabland features are hard to measure with the naked eyes when viewed from a distance. Even when seen through a telescope that brought the current ripples closer than the mile-plus distance they really were, it was still hard to interpret the undulating landscape as much more than a small group of ripples like those seen in the sand along the shore of a lake.

Then, without the aid of magnification, I spotted a few tiny specks emerging from behind one of these ripples.

"What the heck are those?" I asked my hosts.

"Take a look through the lens again," they replied.

Gazing again through the eyepiece, I could now see that the "specks" were actually members of a herd of elk, their massive 800-pound bodies now revealing just how big these ripples really are. Although appearing as tiny undulations on a sandy shore, each of these hills of sand and boulders forming the West Bar are actually from 8 to 10 yards high and more than 120 yards apart.

Geologists have looked at these prominent current ripples resting 150–250 feet above the Columbia River and surmised by their location that floodwaters here were likely as much as 650 feet deep. Another finding of geologists is that the bar was not deposited here—nor the ripples formed—by typical releases of water from Glacial Lake Missoula. Instead, West Bar is one of a number of pieces of geological evidence supporting the existence of another glacial lake that stretched from the Spokane area all the way west to the northern end of Grand Coulee.

What caused this lake to form was an arm, or lobe, of glacial ice called the Okanogan Lobe, which periodically extended south from Canada and blocked the Columbia River, forming the large body of water they call Glacial Lake Columbia. When this lobe of ice retreated or was overridden by water, a tremendous flood would have flowed to the west, using the Quincy Basin exit points to escape and avoiding the scablands altogether.

The current ripples of West Bar

There were likely multiple floods of Lake Columbia, just as there had been of Lake Missoula. The final one would have come near the end of the last ice age, and its waters would have raised the level of the Columbia by hundreds of feet, helping to create the current ripples we can see there today.

Giant current ripples are found at many locations along the path of ice-age floods, and geologists believe the size of the ripples can be a key to the depth of the water at any given location. Deeper water and more swiftly flowing water is apparently conducive to the formation of larger, more well-defined ripple marks, as found in valleys and canyons of the Columbia and Snake rivers. Ripple marks found throughout flatter, more open areas of scabland terrain (such as in Spokane's West Plains, near the Spokane Airport) tend to be smaller and less well-defined.

32 POTHOLES COULEE

GETTING THERE: For a view of Potholes Coulee, take Highway 281 south from Quincy to 5NW, or White Trail Road. Turn right (west). Follow 3 miles to Quincy Lakes Road and turn left (south). After about 2.5 miles, look for several turnouts for viewpoints of Potholes Coulee. Most require short walks. To reach the Ancient Lakes trailhead from Quincy, take SR 28 west about 4 miles and turn left on White Trail Road. Travel south on this road for 1 mile before taking a right turn on

From the air, Potholes Coulee looks like a tiny tear in the earth, but its footprint is massive. If you include the Quincy Lakes that lie above and east of the cataracts and alcoves, the entire flood feature is comprised of more than 15 square miles of eroded, flood-ravaged earth. Perhaps the key attraction of this coulee is the opportunity for viewing incredibly long drops from amazingly high places. Several trails explore nearly every part of the Potholes Coulee system of lakes, dry falls, and gravel bars. If you're hiking up a narrow trail along the edge of a high drop-off with incredible views all around you, it's possible to become so captivated with those views that you lose your footing or step too the equally romantic Road 9 NW. The road changes to Ancient Lake Road, which you should follow south for about 3.9 miles to its end, where the trail begins. To reach the Dusty Lake trailhead from Quincy, take SR 28 west about 4 miles to Road U NW and travel south on this road 3 miles. Turn left on the gravel Quincy Lake Access Road; 2 miles south of the junction with Road U NW, you will see a trail sign reading "Dusty Lake Trail."

REGULATIONS: Discover Pass required; dispersed camping

close to the edge of a precipice. Being aware of your surroundings at all times is key to having a safe visit.

Ancient Lake Trail

The easiest hike in Potholes Coulee is the Lower Ancient Lake Trail. The upper, or northern, alcove of Potholes Coulee contains Ancient Lake—actually three small lakes close together. The trail starts at the mouth of Potholes Coulee and heads toward basalt cliffs to the east and the lakes that lie at their base. The mostly level 4.6-mile round-trip trail passes by flood bars, giant current ripples, and steep basalt cataract cliffs as it heads for the three bodies of water that make up Ancient Lake.

Dusty Lake Trail

The most challenging of the Potholes Coulee trails is probably the Dusty Lake Trail, which is only a little more than a mile long but has

Phenomenal view of south alcove from the shore of Evergreen Reservoir

an elevation gain of some 400 feet. This means there are many steep trail sections and drop-offs to beware of. The rewards for taking this short but strenuous hike are views of potholes, plunge pools, flood bars, and former flood spillways, all significant geologic features in a very short space of trail.

33 FRENCHMAN COULEE

GETTING THERE: Take I-90 to exit 143, just over 5 miles west of George, and exit to North Frontage Road. Take North Frontage Road about 0.5 mile to Silica Road, then follow that road another 0.5 mile to Vantage Road, which descends into Frenchman Coulee and ends at the Columbia River after about 4.5 miles. To get to the Central Rib trailhead, drive down Vantage Road into the coulee. Pull into a parking area on the left side of the road about 1.5 miles down Vantage Road.

REGULATIONS: Discover Pass required

There are many similarities between the Frenchman and Potholes coulees: Two alcoves with dry cascades at their heads and a central rib of basalt define both of these dramatic flood features, formed when voracious floodwaters ate away as they broke through the western edge of Quincy Basin and poured down across Babcock Bench toward the Columbia River.

Although the footprint of Frenchman Coulee is much smaller than that of Potholes Coulee, it is actually easier to get a picture of the whole coulee and cataracts system here because a paved access road enters at the top of the north alcove, tracks along the center rib, then drops down to the coulee floor and passes by the western edge of the south alcove before ending at a boat landing on the Columbia.

Shortly after your first breathtaking view of the coulee from above the top of the north alcove, you come across the Feathers, a row of basalt fins, on your left, which are popular with area climbers. Pull in to park, and you can take a short hike up to a gap between two of the Feathers, from which you can view a smaller, central alcove to the south.

The view into Frenchman Coulee toward the Columbia River

There are a handful of interesting hikes in and around Frenchman Coulee. Some take you down into the coulee's floor and out onto Babcock Bench, where floodwaters made their final drop into the Columbia. Others take you up a narrow trail along the edge of a high drop-off with incredible views all around you.

Central Rib Trail

One of the most dramatic trails in Frenchman Coulee in terms of the views it offers is also one of the shortest in distance—2 miles or less. This trail climbs up to the central rib of basalt separating the north from the south alcove. This route offers some spectacular views, as well as the experience of walking across the stepping-stone-like tops of some really large basalt columns. There is also the chance to see a few erratic rocks way atop the basalt cliffs, indicating how high the waters must have been at one time. The light-colored basalt erratics were transported here by icebergs floating in the floodwaters; the icebergs came to rest, then melted where the rocks they carried sit today.

From the parking area, take the trail heading south that starts beyond the portable toilet and barricade. (Trust me, the trail gets better from here on out!) Once you are moving away from the parking area, the Central Rib Trail ascends to the top of the high island of basalt, where it quickly branches into a maze of trails, any of which will let you explore the entire summit. As you approach the edge of the cliffs, be very cautious, but take

The Feathers above Frenchman Coulee is a popular destination for climbers.

time to look beneath your feet at the five-sided tops of the huge basalt columns that were exposed by floodwaters several thousand years ago.

34 MOSES LAKE

GETTING THERE: Moses Lake is located just west of the town with the same name. Take I-90 to the town of Moses Lake; various access points to the lake itself can be found along I-90 and SR 17. You can view the dunes by taking I-90 to exit 174 at Blue Heron Park, about 2 miles west of town, then head south on a gravel road following signs to the Grant County Off Road Vehicle area.

Moses Lake, like the coulee with the same name, was named after Chief Moses, leader of the Sinkiuse tribe from 1859 to 1899. The lake consists of three main arms more than 18 miles long and up to 1 mile wide. It is the largest natural body of freshwater in Grant County, with more than 120 miles of shoreline covering 6,500 acres. Moses Lake has boat launches and is a popular fishing lake for perch, crappie, walleye, and trout.

As you approach Moses Lake from either the east or west along I-90, its serpentine body seems oddly out of place in this arid,

Moses Lake as seen from Blue Heron Park

largely flat terrain surrounding it. The lake was not directly formed by the ice-age floods; indeed, this is the only natural lake in all of eastern Washington that was not carved out by the turbulent action of the floods.

So how did this popular recreational lake get here? Geologists believe the lake was formed some 4,000 to 6,000 years after the last of the ice-age floods. South of Grand Coulee is the Ephrata Bar—or Ephrata Fan, as some call it (see #27 in chapter 6). This gently sloping terrain is composed of all manner of material that washed through Grand Coulee during the floods. The sands and gravels and rocks were deposited here over a period of several thousand years of flooding and range from boulders to gravel, to sand and fine silt.

In the years following the last flood, the prevailing westerly winds began to remove and redistribute the lighter materials by blowing them to different locations east of the Ephrata Bar. The silt was blown all the way to the region we now call the Palouse, lying along Washington's eastern border with Idaho, where hills of rich soils now grow crops of wheat, barley, lentils, and peas. The sands, however, weighed more than the fine silts that now make up the Palouse soil. The sands dropped out of the westerly winds much closer to their source and became large fields of dunes, most of them south and west of where Moses Lake (both the town and lake) now lie.

Crab Creek flowed from the north through this area and south through the Drumheller Channels area. Over time, the sand dunes began to drift across its path and the creek began to back up, forming the body of water that is now called Moses Lake. The sand dunes have settled down some these days and are popular for off-road vehicle races and sightseeing as well (see the Moses Lake–Quincy Basin Auto Tours). Their large content of basalt makes them much darker in color than the tan-colored dunes we are used to seeing in the desert Southwest.

35 POTHOLES RESERVOIR

GETTING THERE: Potholes Reservoir is south of I-90; it is best accessed by taking SR 17 south from Moses Lake for about 9 miles, then turning right (west) on O'Sullivan Dam Road. At a point some 11 miles west from the junction of SR 17 and O'Sullivan Dam Road is Potholes State Park, the best access to the Potholes Reservoir.

REGULATIONS: Discover Pass required

Just a few miles south of the southernmost arm of Moses Lake is another large body of water, Potholes Reservoir, some 20,000 acres in size. This lake had a completely artificial conception, a result of the 1949 construction of O'Sullivan Dam (one of the largest earthen dams in the United States). The Potholes Reservoir (also referred to as O'Sullivan Reservoir) is the site of Potholes State Park and private resorts along its shores. The 20,000-acre reservoir is popular for water-skiing, boating, swimming, and fishing.

Two interesting things happened when the reservoir was formed. First, a large area of sand dunes southwest of Moses Lake became flooded. The peaks of the tallest dunes still break the surface of the reservoir and have become sandy islands, numbering in the hundreds and making for an otherworldly vision of islands that appear to float atop the lake.

The second occurrence as a result of the construction of O'Sullivan Dam and creation of Potholes Reservoir was that several square miles of the remarkable Drumheller Channels were flooded and drowned forever. The portion that remains—south of the dam—is a scenic and dramatically

Drumheller Channels overlook the serene waters of Potholes Reservoir.

chaotic collection of flood channels and ragged basalt buttes and cliffs, but it is much smaller an overall area now than before the dam was built.

Potholes Reservoir is often confused with the Pothole Lakes themselves, a collection of small, natural pothole lakes about a 30- to 45-minute drive from the state park. The prevailing terrain here is desertlike in appearance but with plentiful freshwater marshes. Around the Potholes Lakes area are sand dunes, rocky canyons, and dozens of lakes.

The desert area of Potholes Reservoir attracts visitors because there is so much water here for recreational uses, all within a fairly small geographical footprint. The reservoir's dune islands are an extension of the sand dunes found south of Moses Lake and prized by all-terrain vehicle and dune buggy drivers. Thousands are attracted to Potholes State Park area each year for camping, swimming, boating, water sports, fishing, hunting, bird-watching, and sunshine. Potholes Reservoir has boat launches and is a popular fishing lake for perch, crappie, walleye, and trout.

Paddling at Potholes State Park

This 640-acre park has 6,000 feet of freshwater shoreline on Potholes Reservoir (also known as O'Sullivan Reservoir). The lower half is not the best paddling water, with powerboats and water-skiers and fishing parties to deal with. But paddlers can head north, hugging the west shore, where they'll eventually reach the maze of sand-dune islands that fill the northern half of the reservoir. The area is a real labyrinth, and it is entirely possible to temporarily lose yourself while paddling around the hundreds of dune islands. Washington State Parks fees may apply.

36 DRUMHELLER CHANNELS

GETTING THERE: Because of the size and intricacy of the area, directions are given for each lake or trail rather than for the Drumheller Channels in their entirety.
REGULATIONS: Discover Pass required; access to wildlife breeding areas restricted during some months; boats allowed only on specified lakes

The Drumheller Channels, which are now part of Columbia National Wildlife Refuge, have changed somewhat since those summer days in the 1920s when J Harlen Bretz tromped through here with a handful of students while conducting his ice-age flood research. The major change was the construction of O'Sullivan Dam in 1949. One of the largest earth-filled dams in the country, it was designed to catch and store the return flow of irrigation waters in the vast Columbia Plateau agricultural area.

Two things happened when this dam was built, however. First, the Potholes Reservoir formed, drowning the northern part of the Drumheller Channels, some 20 square miles in all. Second, the presence of the reservoir raised the water table to the south, causing many formerly dry channels and potholes to fill with water. These water sources were what began to attract migrating waterfowl and other animals, eventually prompting the creation of Columbia National Wildlife Refuge.

Due to the rise in the water table after the building of O'Sullivan Dam, there are sights to be seen today that would not have been here in such abundance during Bretz's time—chiefly, the wildlife drawn here due to the presence of water. The biggest attraction to those who enjoy watching wildlife are the birds—some 100,000 of which can populate the area during some times of the year. Waterfowl return in great numbers from their southern migration spots as winter turns to spring. Most of these are ducks—chiefly gadwalls, mallards, redheads, cinnamon and blue-winged teals, and ruddies. Nesting coots also make this their home and are especially fun to watch, given their belligerent and sometimes comical nature.

The variety of birds found here seems endless. Geese, shrikes, sandhill cranes, great blue herons, northern harriers, black-crowned night herons, American kestrels, red-tailed hawks, long-billed curlews, avocets, bitterns, tundra swans, and others nest and feed here in spring and fall months.

Mammals in the Drumheller Channels area are more secretive and not as easily viewed as birds, but the region is home to a number of warm-blooded creatures such as marmots, muskrats, coyotes, mule deer, beavers, bobcats, and badgers. The cold-blooded have their representatives as well. Lizards and snakes abound, notably the western rattlesnake, which fortunately makes itself scarce and is generally encountered only by those poking around the base of basalt buttes or hiking over talus piles.

The loss of a large portion of the Drumheller Channels to the Potholes Reservoir was regrettable, but the raising of the water table and the subsequent arrival of so many birds, mammals, and reptiles has clearly added a touch of life to a formerly lifeless landscape. And, despite the additional wildlife, a hike through the remaining section of channels provides an experience much like that experienced by Bretz in the 1920s.

My own initial excursion to the Drumheller Channels took place on a sunny Saturday in August, and—given the advance knowledge that hiking, fishing, bird-watching, and even boating were activities that the region was known for—I was amazed that over a period of five hours or more, I saw just two other people and one vehicle. This is still wild and lonesome country, a fact that is realized quickly when you park your car, get out, and set out across the terrain on foot.

As you make your way to any of a thousand plateau tops in the Drumheller Channels and look down at the jumbled channels, deep potholes, and little water pockets below you, it is difficult not to picture a rapid and chaotic flow of water passing through the channels, carving away the basalt as it moves roughshod over the landscape. Because we are so accustomed to seeing rivers neatly contained within their banks and streams following their courses in orderly fashion, it defies ordinary logic to envision what really happened here.

Within the 8- to 12-mile-wide flood path here are hundreds of channels, and it is inside these channels that we imagine the water to have flowed. But it was not *inside* the channels so much as *over* them—in some cases, several hundred feet above the channels—that the waters from the Glacial Lake Missoula floods gushed across the terrain. And it was well beneath the surface of the floods that the carving and scraping was taking place. Had people been able to scramble up to some viewpoint high above the level of the floods, such as up in the Frenchman Hills, they would have seen a broad, torrential river of floodwater several miles wide, with absolutely no features of the landscape visible at all.

The view of the topography of this great geological landmark from the summit of any craggy basalt ridge one may care to scramble up enhances the already powerful sensation it gives off as being a wilderness area worthy of both respect and caution. From such a vantage point, the utterly bewildering nature of the channels, which twist and turn, start and stop throughout this region, becomes evident. From a vantage point of a few hundred feet high or more, it is possible to use your finger to begin charting a course through the bottomland passages below you. But like some schoolboy's baffling maze scribbled in pencil on the back of a sheet of homework, the chosen paths inevitably dead-end, branch into two or three other passages, or lead you directly into a flooded pothole or towering basalt bluff.

And if the task of planning a route seems difficult from above, it is really quite impossible when you are down in the channels themselves. Attempting to cross this landscape in a straight line from point A to B proved all but impossible when I tried it. The channels I selected as trails would suddenly end, divide, or change direction for no apparent reason, thwarting any attempt to walk in a straight line across the scabby basalt ground. Adding to the challenge was the knowledge that as I hiked through this rough terrain, I had been forewarned to be on constant guard for any members of the six species of snakes found in the region.

Fortunately, for those who prefer to stay in their car and avoid a trek on foot, a small number of roads thread through the wildlife refuge and offer some representative geological vignettes of the landscape. From points atop O'Sullivan Dam and along the eastern end of the Frenchman Hills, you can gain some good views of the ragged butte and basin topography that characterizes this region.

When I first visited the Drumheller Channels, I didn't know which roads heading out of the small town of Othello would lead me to my destination. I stopped at a fast-food place, bought a large drink, and asked for directions. The drink was delivered with expertise, but directions were not forthcoming because nobody in the place—including the owner—had ever heard of Drumheller Channels, let alone knew how to get there. At the time, it seemed a bit strange that a local business owner would have no idea that an internationally significant geological region lay within 10 miles of his business. Since that day, however, I have begun to expect a certain lack of awareness on the part of people who live in these areas, regardless of how impressive a nearby geological region might be. After all, does a flood-carved landscape affect their business? Will it bring in more customers? Is there any economic incentive for them to be aware of this place? If not, then maybe it's not always worth knowing about, visiting, or referring others to.

Drumheller Channels near Frog Lake Trail

But maybe that's for the better, and it no doubt accounts for my seeing so few people and cars in this wonderfully wild place in the middle of the Channeled Scablands. After my day-long visit to Drumheller Channels, I considered dropping back by the burger joint to tell them I had found my destination, but I decided the effort would not be worth it. Likely, nobody who worked there would really care for directions to this incredible marvel of nature. And if at some point they decided they did want to visit the place, they could figure out how to get there themselves.

This remarkable area of buttes and channels is rife with potholes, mesas, cataracts, and spillways. Even though you can get a feel for this unique and complex terrain without ever leaving your vehicle, I highly recommend that you venture out to explore the region on foot, as Bretz and his students did some ninety years ago. Some cross-country travel is permitted by personnel of Columbia National Wildlife Refuge, who oversee the Drumheller Channels portion of the refuge. A short distance up Morgan Lake Road, the Columbia National Wildlife Refuge employee facility is on your right; there isn't always anyone on duty here, but if the facility is unstaffed when you drive by, there should at least be a receptacle by the office building that holds maps and brochures of the area. Be sure to grab one of these to help you get around inside the refuge. A less taxing means to get the feel of the landscape than cross-country walking is to take one or more of the half dozen or so trails that cross this flood-ravaged terrain. Two of the best are the Frog Lake Trail and the Upper Goose Lake Trail.

Upper Goose Lake Trail

A great hike within the Drumheller Channels is the Upper Goose Lake Trail. It is a good one to follow to see several large potholes and other flood-eroded basins, a hanging coulee, and a large scabland lake.

To reach the Upper Goose Lake trailhead from O'Sullivan Dam, follow SR 262 (O'Sullivan Dam Road) across the dam, then look for the Mardon Resort on the right (north) side of the highway. At Milepost 14, on the left (south) side of the highway, you will see a gravel road with a "Public Fishing" sign. Follow this down about 1.5 miles into the flood channel below the dam and park at the boat launch for Blythe Lake. The trailhead starts at a locked gate up the hill from the boat launch. The established 2.3-mile trail (one-way) alternates between an old double-track jeep trail and single-track foot trail. At a T intersection about 1 mile into the hike, take the left fork. The trail ends at a viewpoint above Goose Lake. At this point, you can either retrace your steps to the parking lot alongside Blythe Lake, or you can return by a fainter trail that heads in a straight northerly direction and reconnects with the original trail in less than a mile. This alternate route takes you alongside several deep and impressive potholes formed by the tornadolike underwater action during the ice-age floods that passed through here. The only obstacle you'll encounter by following this alternative "nontrail" trail is one short barbed-wire fence you must carefully climb over.

Paddling Upper and Lower Goose Lakes

The deep, canyonlike setting of these lakes almost lets you pretend you're in Arizona floating in some hidden arm of a reservoir filled with Colorado River water—except that the canyon walls are basalt, not sandstone. Goose Lake is outside the boundaries of Columbia National Wildlife Refuge. A Discover Pass is required.

To reach the lake access, from Othello on SR 26, take McManamon Road north about 5.5 miles, then turn right (north) on Morgan Lake Road for about 4 miles. At a T intersection, look for a sign for Goose Lake and turn left. The road ends at the lake access in about 0.75 mile.

Upper Goose Lake is about 1 mile long, and at its south end a narrow 0.5-mile-long channel connects the lake with Lower Goose Lake, an even narrower lake with one arm extending to the west. The seclusion of this place is tangible, and you'll feel as though you've managed to trade contemporary life for a minimalist existence in a hidden world of water, rock, and sky.

Frog Lake Trail

This is a moderate hike of less than 3 miles with a slight elevation gain as you ascend a mesa and gain some breathtaking views of the surrounding buttes, pothole lakes, and flood-ravaged scabland all around you.

To reach the trailhead, from Othello on SR 26, take McManamon Road north about 5.5 miles, then turn right on Morgan Lake Road, the southern access road to the wildlife refuge and Drumheller Channels. Another 3.5 miles will bring you to the trailhead for the Frog Lake hike and a few other hiking trails.

The trail circles around Frog Lake, a small pond surrounded by marshy ground and cattails, then strikes out across open ground as it heads for a ragged butte, then zigzags up to the tablelike mesa on top. The trail then makes a loop around the edges of the plateau, from which you can see pot-hole lakes, flood channels, and other buttes like the one you stand atop.

Paddling Hutchinson and Shiner Lakes

Two of the best lakes for exploring by canoe or kayak are the connected lakes Hutchinson and Shiner. This is technically one lake with a very narrow and shallow connecting passage between the east and west bodies of water. The main attraction, at least to people like me, is the solitude always found here. This is not due to any defects on the part of the lakes but, rather, the limitations placed on visitors by the US Fish and Wildlife Service. In other words, this is one of those places where the list of what you can't do is a great deal longer than the list of things you *can* do. Examples:

You can't camp here. You can't swim here. You can't use gas-powered boats here. You can't hunt here. You can't come here between October and March.

You *can* fish here, but there are no trout; there are bass and bluegill, however.

And there is that sense of seclusion that seems to go so well with the isolated location, the narrow paddleways, and the feeling of enclosure brought about by the walls of cracked and lichen-encrusted basalt columns that flank the shores of these lakes.

To reach the put-in, from Othello on SR 26, take McManamon Road north and west about 8.5 miles and turn left (south) on Hutchinson Lake Road, driving about 1 mile to the lake's shore. For more details, see *Paddle Routes of the Inland Northwest* (see Recommended Resources).

These are not big lakes. From the put-in location at the end of Hutchinson Lake Road to the far end of Shiner Lake, it's barely more than 1.5 miles. But distance paddled should not be the objective. This is a place for leisurely exploration of a water-filled flood channel offering exquisite scabland scenery, sights, and sounds. Aside from the striking basalt walls, your senses can take in a mirrorlike lake surface, aromatic sagebrush-filled meadows, and a colorful display of wildflowers each spring. Add to these elements the sounds of honking geese, quacking ducks, and shrill cries of cliff swallows as they soar around their communal nesting site at the higher levels of the basalt cliffs they call home. I'd call that a perfect day on the water.

37 LOWER CRAB CREEK

GETTING THERE: Because access to this creek is scattered over such a wide area, directions for access follow the description of the paddle trip given below.

REGULATIONS: Ownership of land adjacent to Crab Creek varies—take a good map.

The stretch of Crab Creek in the Quincy Basin area is the final leg of its 163-mile journey from its beginnings east of Reardan (off US 2 in Lincoln County) to its junction with the Columbia River near Beverly. If this seems a rather long distance for a creek to run, consider that Crab Creek is sometimes referred to as the longest ephemeral stream in North America.

This was a major flood channel that caught and confined some of the ice-age floodwaters between the Frenchman Hills and Saddle Mountains after they had passed through the Drumheller Channel area, directing them west toward the Columbia River. The steep, eroded slopes of the Saddle Mountains here on their north flanks show the degree to which raging floodwaters cut away at the mountains as they passed through here.

Given that Crab Creek's various branches run all through the Telford–Crab Creek Tract of scabland and parts of the Moses Lake–Quincy Basin area, it makes sense to paddle through at least one section of this ever-present scabland stream. The problem is that even though the creek runs through three counties and always seems to be within a few miles of where you may happen to be in the scablands, Crab Creek is a fickle little stream, running wildly in some places, moseying along sluggishly in others, and disappearing altogether in spots, such as north of Moses Lake, where it flows underground for several miles.

Pillars from an old bridge make fun obstacles to paddle through.

For this reason, there are really only a handful of places where the creek is navigable and dependably there year-round—and one of them is here in Quincy Basin, near Red Rock Coulee, a small canyonlike passage that captured floodwaters from farther east. These raging waters first flowed west through Natural Corral (an extension of Red Rock Coulee that runs parallel with SR 26), then turned sharply south to follow what was probably an existing stream channel, carrying floodwaters down into Crab Creek Channel.

Paddling Lower Crab Creek

One place where this creek is navigable is the Lower Crab Creek section through the Crab Creek flood channel that runs between the Saddle Mountains and Frenchman Hills.

To reach the put-in off of Road E SW from SR 26, about 5.5 miles west of its junction with SR 262, turn south on Road E SW (the road through Red Rock Coulee). Follow Road E SW about 3 miles until it meets Lower Crab Creek Road and turn right (west), where you can find a place to pull out and park. For a detailed look at the Crab Creek paddle route, see *Paddle Routes of the Inland Northwest* (see Recommended Resources).

Most of the 18-mile floatable route is slow and peaceful, with the high ridges of the Saddle Mountains to your left as you float downstream to the Columbia. In this short segment of navigable water, there is only one small stretch of Class II rapids, which can be avoided by taking out, then walking along the shore beyond the swiftly flowing section.

BRETZ'S CLUES

J Harlen Bretz couldn't help but show enthusiasm when he wrote: "Drumheller is the most spectacular tract of butte and basin scabland on the plateau. It is an almost unbelievable labyrinth of anastomising [braided] channels, rock basins, and small abandoned cataracts." Even Bretz's dramatic statement exhibits some small measure of reserve on his part, since Drumheller Channels have since been recognized by geologists as the most spectacularly eroded area of its size *in the entire world.*

MOSES LAKE–QUINCY BASIN AUTO TOURS

These two tours will give you a feel for the terrain of Quincy Basin and areas around Moses Lake to the east and south of Quincy Basin. They are described as two separate tours because side trips and hikes easily expand each one to a full day, but they can also be combined for one full-day trip of about 185 miles.

 MOSES LAKE–AREA LOOP

This tour starts at Moses Lake, which is east of Quincy Basin but adjoins the area where a deep basin held huge quantities of water that coursed down through the Telford–Crab Creek Tract of scabland and were briefly retained in Quincy Basin before finding exit points to the west and south. Begin this roughly 62-mile loop in the town of Moses Lake on I-90.

Moses Lake: Much of the terrain around Moses Lake is covered with sand dunes. For a side trip to get a good look at some of these gray-toned basalt-rock dunes, from I-90 in Moses Lake take exit 179, head north through town on SR 17 to Road 2 NE and turn left onto it, then turn left (south) onto Road J NE, which becomes Potato Hill Road south of the interstate. On this road, which becomes Sand Dune Road, make the approximately 7-mile loop around the edge of the dune fields and the southern limits of

Moses Lake, circling around back to I-90 at exit 174, about 2.5 miles west of where you began. After your brief tour of the sand dunes, head east back to exit 179 and the junction of I-90 and SR 17.

Potholes Reservoir: Take SR 17 south for about 8.5 miles to O'Sullivan Dam Road (SR 262). Turn right (west) and follow O'Sullivan Dam Road to Road H SE, about 10 miles. While crossing over the dam, you can see part of the Drumheller Channels below you to the left (south), while Potholes Reservoir is on your right (north). Just after crossing the first section of the dam, you'll reach the turnoff for the Upper Goose Lake Trail on your left (see Drumheller Channels below); stop here for a hike if time allows. In another few miles west is the entrance to Potholes State Park on your right, which you might want to visit if time permits. (Discover Pass required at Potholes State Park.)

Drumheller Channels: When you reach Road H SE, turn left (south). Follow this road, which takes you up into the easternmost flank of the Frenchman Hills, for about 1.5 miles until you reach Road I SE. Take this road to the left as it loops around for 2 miles past a scenic overlook of the northwestern section of the Drumheller Channels. Stop here for a great view of potholes, buttes, and channels caused by the torrential floodwaters that flowed through this region. Road I SE rejoins Road H SE about 1 mile farther south from where you left it.

Returning to Road H SE, drive just under 2 miles, then turn left (east) on McManamon Road, crossing Crab Creek and continuing through heavily eroded scabland terrain. Continue following McManamon Road for about 5 miles until you reach Morgan Lake Road. Turn right and head north through the heart of Drumheller Channels. At slightly less than 3.5 miles north of where you turned onto Morgan Lake Road is a turnout for three short trails, including the Frog Lake Trail described earlier in this chapter— another great leg-stretcher if you have the time.

Continuing north on Morgan Lake Road about 1.5 miles, take the right spur road to Soda Lake Dam boat launch and the Pillar-Widgeon trailhead and parking area. Follow this road about 4.5 miles, and soon you return to O'Sullivan Dam Road (SR 262). Head back east to SR 17 in about 6 miles and turn left for the 8.5-mile drive back to Moses Lake to complete the 62-mile loop.

OTHELLO TO TRINIDAD BACK ROADS

This tour starts at Othello on SR 26 and explores the edges of Drumheller Channels and the Frenchman Hills before dropping into the Lower Crab Creek Channel to the Columbia. From there, the 86-mile tour heads north along the east bank of the Columbia to visit Quincy-area features of the Channeled Scablands.

Drumheller Channels: From Othello on SR 26, take McManamon Road north and west about 11 miles to Road H SE and turn right. Follow it about 1.5 miles north to Road I SE. Take this road to the right as it loops around for 2 miles past a scenic overlook of the northwestern section of the Drumheller Channels. Stop here for a great view of potholes, buttes, and channels caused by the torrential floodwaters that flowed through this region. Road I SE rejoins Road H SE about 1 mile farther north from where you left it; continue north on Road H SE about 1.5 miles to O'Sullivan Dam Road (SR 262) and turn left (west). In less than 1 mile is the entrance to Potholes State Park on your right, which you might want to visit if time permits.

Frenchman Hills Erratics: At about 6 miles west of the Potholes State Park turnoff, O'Sullivan Dam Road (SR 262) makes a sharp turn to the left and climbs up to the crest of Frenchman Hills. Just before the road bends, near the junction with Road 7 SW, several boulders lighter than the majority around 'hem can be spotted above on either side of the highway. These rocks are flood-rafted erratics, and the largest is about 8 feet long. As you continue across the Frenchman Hills on SR 262, you pass through some picturesque fruit orchards and in about 6 miles from the Road 7 SW junction intersect with SR 26 a few miles east of Royal City. This tour takes scenic Lower Crab Creek Road on the south side of the creek channel west to SR 243, but if you want to skip that gravel road and shorten the tour, turn right (west) here to take SR 26 to SR 243 a few miles north of Beverly. SR 26 runs east-west along the northern edge of the Crab Creek Channel, which some call Crab Creek Coulee, although there is a flowing stream running down its length.

Lower Crab Creek: To take the gravel road through the Crab Creek Channel, from the junction of SR 262 (the road you took to cross the Frenchman Hills) with SR 26, turn right (west) on SR 26 for about 5.5 miles, then turn left (south) on Road E SW. Follow Road E SW about 3 miles through Red Rock Coulee and across the Crab Creek Channel until the road meets Lower Crab Creek Road. Once you reach Lower Crab Creek Road, turn right (west) and follow the scenic, unimproved road west along Crab Creek, with the towering, flood-eroded slopes of the Saddle Mountains on your left (south).

Saddle Mountains and Sentinel Gap: At about 12.5 miles west of the junction of Road E SW and Lower Crab Creek Road, you'll see a collection of sand dunes climbing up the slope of the Saddle Mountains. These are the Beverly Dunes, and at an off-road vehicle park here you can watch dune buggies and all-terrain vehicles racing around and jumping the dunes. About 2 miles farther west is the small town of Beverly on the Columbia River at the junction with SR 243. To your left at this junction, you can see Sentinel Gap about 1 mile south.

Wanapum Dam: From Beverly, turn right to head north on SR 243. In about 3 miles you will pass Wanapum Dam and Heritage Center, on your left. Here you can tour the dam, watch salmon climbing the fish ladders, and visit exhibits at the heritage center that tell the story of the Wanapum Indian culture.

Wanapum Vista: At about 6 miles north of Beverly, you'll rejoin SR 26, which emerges on your right from the Crab Creek Channel on the north side. This is the road you would have taken if you had not chosen the gravel Lower Crab Creek Road. Another mile farther is the junction with I-90 before it crosses the Columbia at Vantage, making its way west to Seattle. (If time permits, cross the bridge, turn right, and visit the Ginkgo Petrified Forest State Park.) Continuing north on I-90, at just about 1 mile north of its junction with SR 26, there is a scenic overlook called Wanapum Vista. The views here of the Columbia River and its high basalt walls are worth the stop.

Wild Horses Scenic View: Another 0.5 mile up the interstate is the wild-horse sculpture "Grandpa Lets Loose the Ponies," an outdoor art display of several large flat metal wild horses galloping along the cliffs above. The horses were created by sculptor David Govedare, of Chewelah, Washington. Eastbound on I-90, the sculpture is above you and to the right; to see it more easily, continue driving to the Wild Horses Scenic View turnoff about 2 miles north of the Wanapum Vista. You can take a short hike up to view the sculpture up close.

Frenchman Coulee: As you continue eastbound on I-90, it rises to the top of the grade and in another 2 miles north, take exit 143 to North Frontage Road and then Silica Road to visit Frenchman Coulee. Take a hike there, if time permits.

Potholes Coulee: Returning to I-90, continue eastbound from exit 143 just about 5 miles to exit 149 and take Q NW (SR 281) north about 5 miles to 5 NW (or White Trail Road). Turn left after 3 miles onto Quincy Lakes Road to see views of Potholes Coulee after about 2.5 miles.

Crater Coulee; West Bar Ripples: When you return to SR 28 west of Quincy, head another 3 or so miles farther west to Trinidad to see Crater Coulee and the West Bar flood ripples, completing this 86-mile tour.

(To combine the two Quincy Basin tours, take SR 28 east 7 miles back to Quincy and SR 281 south 8.5 miles to I-90, then head east on I-90 28 miles to Moses Lake.)

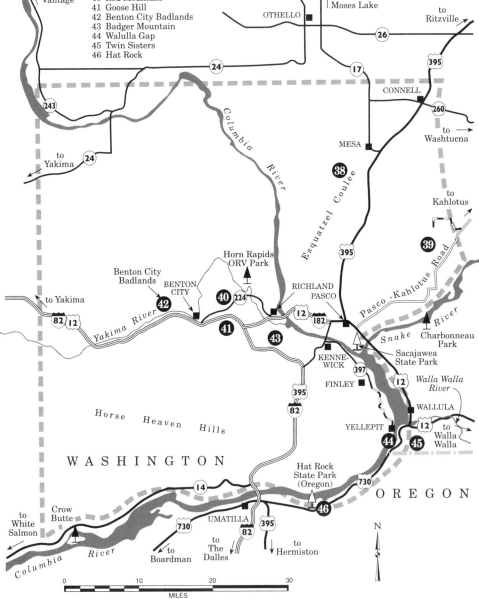

Pasco–Lake Lewis Basins

38 Esquatzel Coulee
39 Juniper Dunes Wilderness Area
40 Red Mountain
41 Goose Hill
42 Benton City Badlands
43 Badger Mountain
44 Walulla Gap
45 Twin Sisters
46 Hat Rock

To Vantage

to Moses Lake

OTHELLO

to Ritzville

26

17

24

CONNELL

243

260

to Washtucna

Columbia River

MESA

to Yakima

24

38

Esquatzel Coulee

395

to Kahlotus

39

Horn Rapids ORV Park

Benton City Badlands

BENTON CITY

RICHLAND PASCO

Pasco-Kahlotus Road

Snake River

to Yakima

42

40

224

12

182

Charbonneau Park

82 12

Yakima River

41

43

Sacajawea State Park

KENNE-WICK

397

12

Walla Walla River

FINLEY

395

WALLULA

82

YELLEPIT

44

45

12

to Walla Walla

Horse Heaven Hills

WASHINGTON

Hat Rock State Park (Oregon)

730

O R E G O N

14

to White Salmon

Crow Butte

UMATILLA

595

46

N

730

82 395

Columbia River

to Boardman

to The Dalles

to Hermiston

0   10   20   30

MILES

Opposite page: *A steep path leads up a Juniper Dunes sand hill.*

EIGHT

PASCO–LAKE LEWIS BASINS

At the eastern edge of the Pasco Basin is the rugged Esquatzel Coulee, a north-south extension of Washtucna Coulee and a pathway for floodwaters that surged swiftly south toward the Tri-Cities area. About 10 miles northeast of Pasco is a bizarre collection of sand dunes and juniper trees in the Juniper Dunes Wilderness Area. Formed by silt that collected on the floor of ice-age Lake Lewis after it had dried up, the dunes are a flood-caused natural feature that nonetheless lie outside of the area of direct flood impact but would not be there had it not been for a monumental ice-age event.

The relatively flat area of land in which the adjoining cities of Richland, Pasco, and Kennewick (known collectively as the Tri Cities) are now located, the Pasco Basin, occupies some 500 square miles that was once the site of a huge ice-age lake, which geologists call Lake Lewis. Floodwaters flowing from northeast to southwest gathered here, slowed by Wallula Gap, a narrow passageway for the Columbia River to negotiate near the Washington–Oregon border west of Walla Walla.

The Pasco Basin is a great place to take a hike up the trails that climb the many low mountains around the urban area and lead to impressive collections of erratic rocks that floated to these locations encased in icebergs. As the water of Lake Lewis receded, the icebergs came to rest, the ice melted, and huge rocks were left high on the slopes of these mountains. Lake Lewis bottom sediment can be observed in many areas of Pasco Basin.

FORMER LAKE LEWIS "ISLANDS"

Given that this corner of eastern Washington was once and repeatedly a massive lake, there are fewer areas of true scablands here, which take rapidly flowing water to form. In fact, many of the most intriguing places to visit in this tract are those that sat above the level of the ancient lake here.

To visit these places, you need to start at a low elevation and climb up to a higher one, to a place where—some 15,000 to 18,000 years ago, you would have been afforded a great view of the massive lake surrounding you. Lake Lewis was as much as 800 feet deep during the largest floods, and its surface level would have been about 1,200 feet above sea level. This means that any physical landforms lower than 1,200 feet in elevation today would have been submerged.

Thus, many of the hikes in the Lake Lewis Basin involve hiking up to the tops of local peaks that stand above 1,200 feet high. The portion of these peaks above 1,200 feet would have been islands in the lake, and it is near the ancient waterlines that some interesting features are often found on the slopes of these high hills (or low mountains, depending on how you look at it).

TOWNS IN THE PASCO–LAKE LEWIS BASINS

- BENTON CITY, on I-82 about 10 miles west of Richland, is a small town of 2,800 located in a fertile, green bend of the Yakima River just before it joins the Columbia. Long Indian summers and moderate winters allow large and small irrigated orchards, vineyards, hayfields, pastures, and acreages to prosper in and around Benton City. Red Mountain vineyards and wineries are to the northeast and Horse Heaven Hills, with its orchards of apple, cherry, pear, apricot, and walnut, is to the southwest. Services include hotels, restaurants, grocery stores, and gas stations.

- CONNELL is located at the junction of US 395 and SR 260, a place that, before 1883, was used by ranchers as open range. The town was founded in 1883 as a junction between the Northern Pacific Railroad and the Oregon Railroad and Navigation Company. Primary businesses here are food processing, agricultural chemicals, and a minimum- and medium-security correctional facility. About 3,000 people live in and near Connell. Services include hotels, restaurants, grocery stores, and gas stations.

- KENNEWICK is located on US 395 along the southwest bank of the Columbia River, opposite Pasco and just south of the confluence of the Columbia and Yakima rivers. Kennewick is the most populous of the three cities known as the Tri Cities (the others are Pasco and Richland), with a population of approximately 68,000. Kennewick has all basic services, from gas stations to restaurants to lodging.

- MESA is located on US 395 at its junction with SR 17. Mesa was originally a stop on the Pasco to Spokane branch of the Northern Pacific Railroad established in 1883. The Columbia Basin Irrigation Project brought water to the area in 1948 and Mesa was officially incorporated on June 23, 1955. Today, Mesa is a small town supported by dryland farming, irrigated farming, and livestock. Basic services include gas stations, restaurants, and grocery stores.

- PASCO is located at the junction of US 395 and US 12, on the north side of the Columbia River between its confluence with the Yakima River to the northwest and the Snake River to the southeast. Pasco, the seat of Franklin County, is one of three cities that make up the Tri-Cities region. Pasco's population is about 56,000. Since the 1990s, Pasco has seen its population overtake the neighboring city of Richland, as growth in retail and tourism industries has boomed. Pasco is home to the Tri-Cities Airport, a regional commercial and private airport. All basic services are found here, from hotels to restaurants, grocery stores to gas stations.

- RICHLAND, one of the Tri Cities, is located at the confluence of the Yakima and Columbia rivers where US 12 splits off from I-82. The city of about 48,000 is gateway to the federal Hanford nuclear site, and it is also the site of Washington State University's Tri-Cities campus. Richland houses technical firms such as the Pacific Northwest National Laboratory, Battelle Memorial Institute, and the CH2M Hill Plateau Remediation Company. The city has all basic services, from gas stations to restaurants to lodging.

PARKS AND CAMPING IN THE PASCO–LAKE LEWIS BASINS

- CHARBONNEAU PARK, off SR 124 along the Snake River, has picnicking, camping, swimming, and boating.

- CROW BUTTE STATE PARK, on SR 14 about 30 miles west of US 395, has picnicking, camping, swimming, boating, and fishing.

- HAT ROCK STATE PARK, on US 730 about 9 miles east of US 395, is in Oregon. It has picnicking, hiking, and boating.

- HORN RAPIDS COUNTY PARK, off SR 225 on the Yakima River, has camping, plus motocross, all-terrain-vehicle, and four-wheel-drive tracks.

- SACAJAWEA STATE PARK, on US 12 just east of Pasco, is day-use only with swimming, boating, and fishing.

38 ESQUATZEL COULEE

GETTING THERE: To view Esquatzel Coulee from US 395 as you travel south, simply look to your right shortly after you have passed Connell, and you'll see its rough basalt walls and the coulee floor a few hundred feet below. Traffic on the highway is generally light enough that it's usually safe to pull over and park at a wide spot along the road, get out, and walk over to where you can get a better view of the Esquatzel vista. In most places, barbed wire fences

In some respects, Esquatzel Coulee is a continuation of Washtucna Coulee, which runs east to west and merges with Esquatzel at the town of Connell. Providence Coulee also terminates at Connell, which is perhaps best known by motorists for its medium-security prison that can be seen from the highway.

Before the first Glacial Lake Missoula floods, the Palouse River flowed west through Washtucna Coulee (which wasn't a coulee at that point), then turned south and flowed down a valley that is now Esquatzel Coulee. The river continued all the way south to the present site of the Tri Cities, joining the Columbia River somewhere near Pasco.

Esquatzel Coulee is almost a moonscape in places.

mark the boundary between state and private land. Respect private property rights, and if you do find a way to get closer to the edge of the coulee, be careful as you would at any location with a sheer drop-off and loose surfaces.

REGULATIONS: Respect property owners' rights and posted signs.

When the floods diverted the Palouse River down the newly carved Palouse Canyon and over Palouse Falls, floodwaters were so intense that they continued west and widened Washtucna "Valley" into a coulee, then flowed south through Esquatzel "Valley," similarly reaming it out. But after each subsequent flood had run its course, the Palouse then followed the channel that had been cut for it through the divide and toward the Snake River. When another flood came, Washtucna and Esquatzel coulees were again filled, then dried out again when the flood was over.

Of the dozens of coulees found in the Channeled Scablands, many have roads running right along their floors, a logical arrangement when the coulee corridor runs in the same direction you'd like your road to travel. In other cases, roads meet coulees at right angles, dipping down into and crossing these channels, then climbing up the other side to head off wherever they are going.

Esquatzel Coulee is one of the few in the scablands with a major highway running right along its edge for the full course of its nearly 20-mile length. As you drive down US 395 south of Connell, Esquatzel Coulee lies to the right (west) and below you, allowing for some great views down into this craggy and picturesque channel that runs north and south. Land along the highway above the coulee is controlled by the state highway department; the floor of the coulee is either privately owned or Burlington Northern Railroad property.

Esquatzel Coulee Hike

This easy hike takes you along the floor of Esquatzel Coulee near the town of Mesa. The trail is located in a wildlife area controlled by the Washington Department of Fish and Wildlife.

To reach the trailhead, at Mesa (about 8 miles south of Connell), leave US 395 and head north on SR 17, turning right on Manton Way. Drive under the highway to a gravel road that crosses railroad tracks. After the tracks, turn right and head into the coulee, passing a grain elevator. When the road splits at another SR 17 overpass, stay to the left; the trailhead is about 0.25 mile ahead. Park at the Esquatzel Coulee Wildlife Area sign. Discover Pass required; respect regulations posted on signs.

This 3-mile round-trip trail offers views of the coulee walls, passes by a large flood-deposited gravel bar, and ends at a small pond.

39 JUNIPER DUNES WILDERNESS AREA

GETTING THERE: From Pasco, follow US 12 south (eastbound) about 2 miles from its junction with US 395, and take the Pasco-Kahlotus Road exit. Follow Pasco-Kahlotus Road north about 5 miles to Petersen Road and take Petersen Road north about 4 miles. A parking area is here at the southwest corner of a large off-road vehicle area, but the Juniper Dunes Wilderness Area is still about 3 miles to the northeast. Continue east on the improved road just over 2 miles to another parking area and information kiosk. The road continues but is unimproved and sometimes covered with windblown sand at this point,

An author of a book about the Channeled Scablands would be remiss if he did not mention the Juniper Dunes Wilderness Area, even though this is not a true ice-age flood feature. By this I mean that it was not directly caused by the floods themselves. This 7,000-acre preserve of sand dunes and old-growth juniper was, however, formed as an indirect result of the floods. Much evidence supports the theory that winds in this corner of Washington State have blown from the southwest since the close of the last ice age, around 15,000 years ago. Because the floods were slowed down by Wallula Gap (see #44), they formed Lake Lewis, a large slackwater lake whose basin was eventually filled with large deposits of sand and silt each time a new flood coursed through the region.

After the last floods, these thick deposits of sand and silt dried out and were baked by so you may need four-wheel drive to continue. Either by vehicle or on foot, follow this unimproved road another 0.75 mile to where the road splits. Take the right fork and continue another 0.8 mile or so to a gate and fencing that indicates the opening to the wilderness area. At this point you are on the southwest edge of the protected area. To use the north entrance (open during March, April, and May only) take Blanton Road east from Eltopia for about 5 miles to Overturf Road. Turn right (east) on Overturf Road and travel a little over 2 miles to Gertler Road. Turn right (south) on Gertler and travel about 3 miles to East Blackman Ridge Road. Turn left (east) and travel about 2 miles to Joy Road. Turn right (south) on Joy Road. Parking area is at end of Joy Road, about 2 miles.

REGULATIONS: No camping; no hiking after dark; respect signs posted by adjoining landowners.

the sun. Then the prevailing winds began to pick up and redistribute these materials. The story here is similar to that of the Ephrata Fan and the sand dunes south of Moses Lake (see Chapter 6, Grand and Moses Coulees). Over thousands of years, the lightest materials blew many miles to the northeast before falling back to the earth and adding to the rich hills of the Palouse agricultural region.

The heavier sands from the Lake Lewis basin did not remain airborne as long as the lighter silts. The sands fell to earth before they had traveled very far—specifically, in the region where the Juniper Dunes lie today. And so, though they were not *created* by the floods, the Juniper Dunes would not be here had the floods not occurred.

Sand dunes here can be as much as 130 feet high and 1,000 feet long. Although many dunes are completely bare of vegetation, many acres of dunes are bedecked with grasses and small junipers, some of which are more than 100 years old, spaced in such a way that it appears almost as if they were planted in rows by some dedicated Johnny Juniperseed.

Much of the area around the protected region of old-growth juniper and scenic sand dunes is open to off-highway vehicles such as four-wheel drives and dune buggies. But the critically delicate area containing groves of the most northerly old-growth junipers in North America is protected and, as such, has been designated as eastern Washington's only wilderness area, accessible solely on foot or horseback. The only danger here—aside from the possibility of losing your way—is the extreme heat in this area during summer and the year-round lack of any water. Spring and fall, or even winter if snow is absent, are the best times to visit this unique region of southeastern Washington.

The north faces of some dunes are grassy, as seen here.

The BLM-administered land has few access points; BLM has an agreement with local landowners to allow access via Peterson Road, off Pasco-Kahlotus Road. There is also limited access certain months of the year from the north, but it is based on an agreement with property owners that could change any time, so the recommended access to this area is from the south.

Juniper Dunes Cross-Country Hike

The Juniper Dunes Wilderness Area can be explored by simply heading off in any direction on foot, but there is a very loose network of trails circling around the dunes and groves of junipers. Keep track of where you are as you set off to explore this unique area of scenic dunes and juniper trees.

BRETZ'S CLUES

In the fall of 1924, J Harlen Bretz published some estimates of the ice-age flood's volume. If the volume could be measured anywhere, he knew it would be at Wallula Gap. Bretz asked mathematician D. F. Higgins to compute a volume for the initial flood "before any noteworthy deepening or widening had lowered its surface." Using an imaginary cross section of the floodwaters rising to 1,025 feet in mid-length of the Wallula Gap, Bretz and Higgins determined that a two-dimensional measurement of the flood's cross-sectional area would be some 3,485,000 square feet.

Bretz and Higgins stated that the volume of the flood could then be obtained by using a formula incorporating the velocity of the floodwaters, hydraulic radius, slope of the surface, and the character of the channel.

Bretz legitimized the formulaic variables by noting in his paper that similar techniques had been "devised for and [are] applied to small-capacity drainage lines, such as sewers, ditches, etc." It almost seems crazy that a formula for measuring "small-capacity drainage lines" could be applied to a catastrophic flood event more than 1,000 feet high, but Bretz knew that flowing water behaves in a certain way no matter what volume is involved.

Higgins and Bretz then proceeded to come up with figures such as velocities (20.6 feet per second at one location, 30.4 feet per second at another), discharge (66,132,000 second-feet, or 38.9 cubic miles per day), and volumes—50 *times* the volume of present-day floods in the Columbia.

40 RED MOUNTAIN

GETTING THERE: To reach the trailhead, from Richland take SR 240 north to Van Giesen Street. Exit and head through West Richland, where Van Giesen becomes SR 224. In about 3.5 miles from West Richland, turn right on Red Mountain Road. After just 0.2 mile, turn left toward a power substation. Parking is on the south side of this facility.

REGULATIONS: No motorized vehicles

Red Mountain is a narrow basalt ridge about 3 miles long standing at about 1,400 feet above sea level. At the 1,200-foot line, there are dozens of erratic rocks, most of them granite (see sidebar). Not all erratic rocks are found precisely at the highest levels of a glacial lake like Lake Lewis. Some icebergs would lodge against an island, then drop somewhat in elevation as the lake level dropped, eventually coming to rest atop a horizontal bench or shelf of the hill. So erratic rocks can be found at the highest water level (1,200 feet) and below. This is true along the trail up to the top of Red Mountain, where erratics as low as 600 feet are found. The trail area is jointly owned by Washington State Department of Natural Resources, Kennewick Irrigation District, and Bonneville Power Administration.

The territorial view from the trailhead at Red Mountain

Red Mountain Trail

Like most of the hiking trails on the former Lake Lewis "islands" in this area, the Red Mountain Trail is fairly strenuous, with an elevation gain of more than 800 feet in about a 3-mile one-way hike. The Red Mountain Trail starts at about 600 feet and takes you to the top of Red Mountain at 1,410 feet. As you begin hiking the trail, stay to the south to keep off adjoining private land. Along the trail up to the top of Red Mountain, you'll first begin seeing erratics as low as the 600-foot level. The highest erratics are at the 1,200-foot level.

41 GOOSE HILL

GETTING THERE: To reach the Goose Hill trailhead, from Richland take I-182 west to I-82 and head west to the Benton City exit. From the exit head south, passing under the interstate, to Jacobs Road, which runs parallel to I-82. Head east on Jacobs and drive just a

Now at 1,339 feet in elevation, Goose Hill rose just 139 feet above the highest level of former Lake Lewis. Along the Goose Hill Trail, you will pass by a plentiful number of erratic rocks, some alone and others in tightly spaced clusters. Geologists believe these to be rocks that were rafted in together as a group in one iceberg. When the iceberg melted, all the rocks were released at the same spot,

Plenty of sagebrush to see from the Goose Hill Trail

few tenths of a mile to Field Road. Parking is available at the point where Field and Jacobs Roads intersect.

REGULATIONS: No motorized vehicles

where they remain today. At the top of Goose Hill (owned by Washington State Department of Natural Resources), you will be rewarded by a great view to the west. From the summit you can see the Yakima River, Horse Heaven Hills, and a scabland tract near Benton City called the Badlands.

Goose Hill Trail

The moderately strenuous trail to the top of this former island features an 840-foot gain in about 2.5 miles one-way. From the parking area, the old four-wheel-drive road heads to the top of Goose Hill. As you move along the trail, you'll pass by plenty of erratics. From the top of the hill, the trail continues for a bit down the east side of the hill, where it ends. When you're done looking around, retrace your steps back to the trailhead.

42 BENTON CITY BADLANDS

GETTING THERE: To see a section of the badlands terrain, from I-82 take the Benton City exit, then head north for about 0.5 mile

When floodwaters were backed up at Wallula Gap during each ice-age flood event, they flowed through the lower Yakima Valley area near Benton City, west of the Tri Cities, where the Yakima River flows today. First, the water flowed from east to west

Benton City Badlands are a jumbled maze of basalt boulders.

through Benton City, turning left on the Old Inland Empire Highway. After about 4 miles, start looking for the large basalt boulders scattered about primarily on the north side of the road. They reach their maximum at about 5 miles from Benton City. There are a few places where you can pull out and park, then get out on foot to explore these large boulders that tumbled down here from the cliffs above.

as the floods came through; then, as the waters of Lake Lewis all drained through Wallula Gap, the water in the Yakima Valley retreated back to the east again. Because this section of the little valley was narrow then, as it remains today, the water must have reached high velocities when it shot through here as if from a fire hose.

For every flood that flowed through Wallula Gap, there were two rushes of water through this narrow section of the Yakima Valley, first flowing from east to west, then from west to east again. In the process, the floodwaters washed away the topsoil and carved away at the basalt beneath. The result is an area of potholes, rock benches, and standing boulders that rolled down from the tops of the exposed basalt cliffs with each subsequent flood.

43 BADGER MOUNTAIN

GETTING THERE: To reach the Badger Mountain trailhead, from Richland take I-182 west to Queensgate South (exit 3A). Travel 0.5 mile to Keene Road,

Badger Mountain is the latest of the former Lake Lewis "islands" to be opened for hiking. A few years ago, a local conservation campaign worked to create what is now

The popular Badger Mountain Trail overlooks a burgeoning neighborhood.

then drive about 0.6 mile to Shockley Road. Shockley becomes Queensgate. Park at the City of Richland's Badger Mountain Park, and walk to the trailhead at the top of a small hill. For those traveling with canine members of the family, it's worth noting that Badger Mountain Park has a dog park as well.

REGULATIONS: No biking, horseback riding, or motor vehicles

called the Badger Mountain Centennial Preserve, owned by the city of Richland and Benton County. During the largest of the ice-age floods, the 1,580-foot mountain stood about 300 feet above the highest level of glacial Lake Lewis. It is at the top of this and other Lake Lewis "islands" that you can really get a mental picture of this region as a onetime glacial lake. On clear days, you can also see the peaks of Mount Hood and other snow-covered mountains in the Cascade Range to the west.

Badger Mountain Trail

A 3.4-mile round-trip trail leads to the summit and back. The short but strenuous hike takes you past numerous erratic rocks as it winds its way to the summit, where spectacular views of the Pasco Basin and other Lake Lewis islands can be seen.

44 WALLULA GAP

GETTING THERE: Viewing Wallula Gap is possible all along US 12 north of the gap and from US 730, which runs right through the gap itself and on into Oregon. Some of the best places to take photos of Wallula Gap are along the river near the town of Wallula, at the mouth of the Walla Walla River as it empties into the Columbia, and almost anywhere along US 730 as you pass into Oregon.
REGULATIONS: Obey posted signs.

If there is a Holy Grail, a Magna Carta, a Mecca to ice-age flood enthusiasts, it is most likely the narrow passageway through which the Columbia River flows at a point just north of where Oregon and Washington states adjoin. This is a special place and integral to the ice-age floods story for several reasons. But first, here's a brief description of this place called Wallula Gap.

Reduced to its basic elements, Wallula Gap consists of a pair of basalt cliffs, one on each side of the Columbia as it makes its final bend to the west, just a few miles north of where the river creates the line separating Oregon from Washington. There is no hard and fast delineation marking the beginning or end of the gap, or Gateway, as it was more often called in J Harlen Bretz's time. But give or take a few dozen yards, the gap is about 10 miles long, often defined as the space between River Mile 304 and 314. (A river mile designates the distance from the mouth of a river to a point upstream.) The width of Wallula Gap at its narrowest point is about 0.75 mile. Remember, however, that before McNary Dam was completed in 1954 at Umatilla, Lake Wallula had not yet been formed, which has widened the river here. This means that the river used to be even narrower at Wallula Gap than it is now.

The elevations of the cliffs that form the gap are 1,160 feet on the west side and 1,340 feet on the east side. Both of these measurements sound high, but they actually represent the lowest elevations of the basalt cliffs along this stretch of the river. From the edge of the cliffs where these heights were calculated, the elevation increases: from 1,160 to 1,430 feet 1.5 miles away from the cliffs on the west side, and from 1,340 to 1,560 feet 1.5 miles away from the cliffs on the east side. This down-sloping geological configuration had a great deal to do with the way floodwaters passed through here.

Back in the early 1920s, J Harlen Bretz could see that the narrow gap had clearly been a major constriction during the ice-age floods. (Back in the 1920s, Bretz believed there was a single flood, but he accepted a multiflood scenario when it was suggested by other geologists decades later.) Bretz had already imagined floodwaters more than a few hundred feet high as he was developing his theory, but when he and his graduate students hiked up to the top of Wallula Gap in 1923, they encountered scabland terrain atop the basalt cliffs. Formation of scabland requires swiftly running water, and so Bretz also began developing his hypothesis that scabland was formed under deep water by the tornadolike action of currents far beneath the surface of a flood.

So, as unbelievable as it seemed even to Bretz—who had first come up with the flood theory—he knew after only a few trips to the Wallula Gateway site that floodwaters had been so constricted by the narrow gap that the water had risen up to and *above* the tops of the cliffs at the crest of Wallula Gap.

Given the depth of the normal Columbia River and the height of the cliffs above the river, this meant the river had flowed at a level well above that of the cliffs at Wallula Gap. Not only did the evidence of scabland at more than 1,000 feet above the river embolden Bretz during his first few years of field research, but it led him to compile additional theoretical commentary regarding other flood features that could be more easily explained now, given a massive lake behind Wallula Gap. He now envisioned a lake that backed water up the Columbia River, up the Snake River, and into flood-carved channels such as Washtucna Coulee (see #10 in chapter 4).

When you visit Wallula Gap, you should view it from both north and south, as well as drive through it on US 730. Imagine, as Bretz no doubt did, the massive, almost explosive wall of water that would have burst through this gap during a flood event, rising so high that it overflowed the lofty

The west side of Wallula Gap near Twin Sisters

cliffs of basalt and flowed across their plateau tops before cascading back down into the Columbia on the other side.

Wallula Gap, then, figures prominently in the look of the landscape here, the course taken by the floods, and the development of the flood theory by Bretz. The geological significance of the region was recognized by the National Natural Landmarks Program, which has designated Wallula Gap as a Natural Landmark.

Beyond the obvious geological and ice-age floods components of Wallula Gap, however, other aspects of this unusual place cause it to be considered special by many who know it best. Robert J. Carson and Lawrence L. Dodd put it nicely in the introduction to their book, *Where the Great River Bends*:

"Wallula Gap is an oasis in the desert of eastern Washington and Oregon. From end to end, and top to bottom, there are only two residences. The vegetation immediately adjacent to water (for example, in Juniper Canyon) differs completely from the rest of the vegetation. Wallula Gap is part of a desert, yet there are beavers. Wallula Gap has no mountains, yet there are bighorn sheep. The bedrock is all basalt, yet there are granite boulders."

If you have the opportunity to see Wallula Gap only from the highways along the river, you will still get a good idea of the major constriction it represented to the Columbia River during times of overwhelming ice-age flooding from Glacial Lake Missoula. Because Wallula Gap is an extended landscape feature covering several square miles, different access points have different landowners. Obey posted signs, and if you hike to the top of Wallula Gap, be very cautious of sheer drops.

Wallula Gap Hike

To get a really great impression of the height those ice-age floodwaters would have risen, a hike to the top of Wallula Gap is a must. Total distance from the trailhead at 360 feet elevation to an overlook at about 1,160 feet elevation is about 3.2 miles, nearly 800 feet in elevation gain. As you work your way to the top of the cliffs overlooking the river some 800 feet below, you will see erratic boulders of granite that were ice-rafted to these heights, a hanging coulee, basalt rocks littering the tops of the cliffs, and some remarkable views you will never forget.

To reach the trailhead, from Kennewick travel southeast on SR 397, driving through the town of Finley. About 7 miles south of Kennewick, SR 397 turns into Piert Road. Continue south on Piert Road for about 1 mile, then veer left on Meals Road, taking it another 4.5 miles and then turning left onto Ayers Road. Follow this gravel and dirt road about 2.2 miles to Yellepit, where the road ends. Here is a locked gate and a four-wheel-drive road that heads uphill.

From the locked gate at the trailhead, take the old road, bearing right after 0.4 mile, then heading up a canyon with a steep section at about 0.8 mile after you veered right. At 1 mile from the trailhead, you'll encounter a fence and gate. Don't go through the gate, but follow the trail heading up the hill (south). Other trails cross the one you are following as you make your way up the hill. Continue in a south-southeast direction toward the top of the bluff, and at about 2.5 miles from the trailhead, you should see a 5-foot-long granite erratic, rafted here via iceberg during a glacial flood.

Just less than another 0.3 mile brings you to an incredible overlook down into Wallula Gap. (There is a radio tower here.) If you hike another 0.6 mile south, you'll arrive at an even more dramatic view of the gap and the river below you.

Do the math. The top of Wallula Gap is more than 1,100 feet high. That's more than 760 feet above the Columbia River. Enjoy your hike to the top, but when you get there, stay a safe distance away from the edge. And please don't say to anyone whose picture you are taking, "Just step back a few more feet . . ."

45 TWIN SISTERS

GETTING THERE: From the Tri Cities, take US 12 south 16 miles to Wallula Junction. At the junction, take US 730 south 1.9 miles to the abrupt turnout. Keep an eye on your odometer, because the

One of the most recognized geological landmarks in the Wallula Gap region is a flood-ravaged basalt monolith in the shape of two towers about 100 feet high along US 730, less than 2 miles south of the junction with

US 12 (to Walla Walla). This eroded chunk of basalt figures large in Native American legend, with its name Twin Sisters or Two Sisters coming from a legend of Coyote and his two wives whom he turned to stone when he became jealous of them. Over the past hundred years, the two pillars have been called everything from Twin Captains to Two Virgins and Castle Rocks to Hell's Smoke Stacks.

turnout is around a blind curve and is easily missed. Pull into the small parking area and look for the trail beginning on the other side of a barbed wire fence.

The very scenic basalt landmark is frequently photographed but is often passed right by because the turnout for the small parking area below the towers comes into view very abruptly around a bend in the highway. If you manage to pull off here, use caution when re-entering traffic on the highway. Safely leaving the parking area around the blind corner can be as challenging as finding it in the first place.

Twin Sisters Hike

At the parking area, a short ladder allows you to climb over the barbed wire fence to the other side. Walla Walla County owns the land on which the Twin Sisters and the trail are located; land to the north and east is privately owned, so stay on the trail. The hike to the base of the towers is only 0.2 mile, but there is a fairly good elevation gain in that short distance. The short trail climbs 200 feet up the basalt talus slope to the middle of the two towers. One of the best reasons for scrambling up this short but steep trail is for the views it offers of Wallula Gap from the top of the trail.

The Twin Sisters dominate the landscape from any direction.

46 HAT ROCK

Like the Twin Sisters, Hat Rock is a basalt remnant of the turbulent erosion caused by glacial flooding. It remained after the last floods had passed. Lewis and Clark passed by this monument and were the first to note its resemblance to a hat.

Hat Rock is on the south (Oregon) shore of Lake Wallula, the lake formed by McNary Dam, in an Oregon state park. The park is a desert oasis surrounded by rolling sagebrush hills and craggy basalt outcroppings. Hat Rock State Park offers a grassy, tree-shaded retreat from summer, and a boat ramp conveniently opens the lake to public use, where anglers fish for sturgeon and walleye. Waterskiing, boating, and swimming are also popular. The park has its own pond—stocked with rainbow trout—and provides year-round habitat for waterfowl.

The view of Hat Rock is framed by lush vegetation.

LAKE LEWIS ERRATICS

All along the ridges of the many hills near Pasco, Richland, and Kennewick, Washington, are large chunks of rocks, many of them granite, which look as if they don't really belong here, because the nearest source for some of these rock types is more than 100 miles away. So how did these rocks—some of them the size of large farm animals—arrive high up on the slopes of the tall hills near the Tri Cities?

Remember that when the Glacial Lake Missoula floods occurred, the earth was nearing the end of a long ice age. Average temperatures were much lower than we know today, and floodwaters would have been a mucky mix of water, mud, ice, tree trunks, and intact icebergs that were as much as many dozens of feet across. (There probably would have been a collection of mammoth, camel, and saber-toothed tiger carcasses as well.) If the icebergs surging along with the floods had been part of the original ice dam—which was actually a lobe, or leading edge, of a glacier—they would likely have been chock full of rocks that had been pushed and collected by the glacial ice as it had moved slowly south across the frigid landscape.

Picture then, a floating iceberg filled with rocks and swept away by floodwaters traveling southwest from what is now northern Idaho. As the rock-filled icebergs moved south, ambient temperatures would have risen slightly, and the ice floating in the floods would have begun to melt. As the icebergs floated around large bodies of water such as Lake Lewis, they would have occasionally brushed up against the shores of the islands formed by the tops of tall hills such as those found west of the Tri-Cities area.

As each flood ended and the level of Lake Lewis dropped, some of the icebergs lodged along the islands' shores and sat there melting. When the ice had completely melted, what was left were the rocks that had been trapped within the ice. And there they wait for us to come upon today as we hike along a number of Lake Lewis "island" trails.

Geologists call these rocks ice-rafted erratics; they traveled far from home and ended high up on the upper slopes of hills, marking the upper limits of the frigid waters that once formed huge, temporary lakes throughout the Pacific Northwest. Incidentally, those mammoth carcasses that rode along with the rocks soon became bones, and some of these bones are found on a regular basis in many of the same spots where the ice-rafted rocks came to rest—chiefly, at elevations of 1,000–1,250 feet, consistent with the highest levels attained by the waters of Glacial Lake Lewis.

PASCO–LAKE LEWIS BASINS AUTO TOURS

Most of the ice-age flood features to be visited in this region involve parking your car and climbing up to a higher place. This means there are fewer areas where scabland geology can be seen right from the windows of your car. A half day's drive around the region, however, will reveal a number of geological sites and give you a better overall impression of the huge lake that existed here temporarily following each ice-age flood from Glacial Lake Missoula. The first loop drive takes in the northeastern part of this region, and the second loop drive visits Wallula Gap; both can be combined, of course, for a longer tour.

 ESQUATZEL COULEE–JUNIPER DUNES LOOP

This 97-mile drive explores the coulee country between Connell and the Tri Cities, taking in the Juniper Dunes Wilderness Area, as well as Devils Canyon and Washtucna Coulee (both described in chapter 4).

Starting in Connell, on US 395, begin your trip by gazing up the mouth of Washtucna Coulee and keeping in mind that the waters from Lake Lewis were deep enough and spread far enough north to pour into this huge coulee and back up water that also poured into Washtucna from the north. This deluge apparently assisted with the process of water overflowing divides in Washtucna Coulee and creating deep gorges such as the Palouse Canyon and Devils Canyon.

Esquatzel Coulee: Also note how Connell sits in a hollow at the junction of Washtucna Coulee to the east and Esquatzel Coulee to the south. Esquatzel was more or less an extension of Washtucna that followed the slope of the landscape and flowed south toward the Pasco Basin. As you follow US 395 south alongside Esquatzel Coulee, look for places to view the coulee's rugged walls and floor from the side of the highway. Or drive 9 miles to Mesa and take the short hike along the coulee's floor.

Juniper Dunes Wilderness Area: From Mesa, continue south on US 395 for 20 miles toward Pasco, then take US 12 east 2 miles to Pasco-Kahlotus Road. Follow this road northeast 5 miles to access the Juniper Dunes Wilderness Area (6 miles to the trailhead), then hike either on trails or cross-country to explore this unusual place.

Devils Canyon: From the wilderness area, return to Pasco-Kahlotus Road and continue northeast about 31 miles toward Kahlotus, stopping at the Devils Canyon overlook (see chapter 4).

Washtucna Coulee: Drive the last mile or so to Kahlotus on SR 260, in the middle of Washtucna Coulee. Turn left onto the highway and take it west 17 miles to Connell to close the loop and complete this 97-mile tour.

TRI CITIES—WALLULA GAP LOOP

This roughly 140-mile loop around the Pasco–Lake Lewis Basins area will give you a much better idea where ice-age floodwaters flowed, where they collected, and how they worked their way out through Wallula Gap to continue their journey west to the ocean. Along the way, you'll have plenty of chances to stretch your legs on one or more of the Lake Lewis "islands" and at viewpoints of Wallula Gap. You can skip any one of these hiking destinations to shorten your journey's miles and time.

Red Mountain: From Richland in the Tri-Cities area, take SR 240 north to Van Giesen Street and head through West Richland (about 5 miles from SR 240 and US 12 in Richland), where Van Giesen becomes SR 224. In about 3.5 miles from West Richland, turn right on Red Mountain Road. After just 0.2 mile, turn left toward a power substation and park on the south side of this facility. After your hike up this Lake Lewis "island," return the 3.7 miles to SR 224 and turn right (west) to drive about 3 miles to Benton City.

Goose Hill: From the Benton City exit off I-82, head south, passing under the interstate, to Jacobs Road, which parallels I-82. Head east on Jacobs Road and drive just a few tenths of a mile to Field Road. Park where Field and Jacobs Roads intersect and enjoy another hike to view iceberg-delivered erratics. After your hike, return about 0.5 mile to Benton City.

Benton City Badlands: From the Benton City exit off I-82, head north for about 0.5 mile through Benton City, turning left on the Old Inland Empire

Highway. After about 4 miles, start looking for the large basalt boulders scattered about primarily on the north side of the road. They reach their maximum at about 5 miles. After exploring, return to Benton City and get on I-82 heading southeast, then take I-182 east to Queensgate South (exit 3A), about 8 miles from Benton City.

Badger Mountain: From the I-182 exit, travel 0.5 mile to Keene Road, then drive about 0.6 mile to Shockley Road; Shockley becomes Queensgate. Park at Badger Mountain Park, and take a walk to the top of Badger Mountain, with views of the Horse Heaven Hills to the south. After your hike, return on Keene Road about 1.1 miles to the Queensgate South exit on I-182, but instead of getting on the interstate, turn right onto Columbia Drive, which becomes SR 240 into Kennewick in 8 miles. Before SR 240 crosses the Columbia into Pasco, turn right onto SR 397.

Wallula Gap: From Kennewick travel southeast on SR 397, following directions earlier in this chapter through Finley to a locked gate at the end of the road at Yellepit in 14.7 miles. Start walking here for the hike up to the view above Wallula Gap. When you've finished gazing, return the way you came, back to Kennewick, and this time cross the Columbia on SR 240 to its junction with US 12 eastbound.

Twin Sisters: Follow US 12 east about 16 miles to Wallula Junction and continue south on US 730 for 1.9 miles to the Twin Sisters, stopping for the short hike up to the top of this formation if time allows.

Hat Rock: Follow US 730 west about 14 miles to Hat Rock State Park, then continue west on the highway to its junction with US 395 at Umatilla in 9 miles. Cross the Columbia heading north to return to the Tri Cities in 26 miles to close the loop for this 140-mile tour.

Opposite page: *Basalt columns located not far from Harrington*

PART III

Future of the Channeled Scablands

NINE
THE ICE AGE FLOODS NATIONAL GEOLOGIC TRAIL

In 2001, the National Park Service (NPS) completed a major Special Resource Study and submitted a report to Congress proposing that an Ice Age Floods National Geologic Trail be established. Such a trail would represent the largest, most systematic, and most cooperative effort yet proposed to bring the dramatic story of the ice-age floods to the public's attention. Counties throughout the Pacific Northwest will benefit because an Ice Age Floods National Geologic Trail has the potential to bring significant economic and cultural advantages to local communities. The National Park Service report was prepared by the firm of Jones and Jones and is available in PDF or HTML format at an NPS website (www.nps.gov/iceagefloods/).

The Ice Age Floods National Geologic Trail will essentially be a network of marked touring routes extending across parts of Montana, Idaho, Washington, and Oregon, with several special interpretive centers located across the region (see the Proposed Ice Age Floods Pathways map).

The Park Service's report indicates that, by bringing together many interested parties, an effective interpretive program can be developed within a collaborative structure and at remarkably low cost, despite the extraordinary size of the region. The trail can also be developed on existing public lands, with no changes in jurisdiction and no threats to private property rights. This alone is an extraordinarily beneficial aspect of the NPS proposal. The role of the National Park Service would be to coordinate and manage the planning of the project and the telling of the story, not to manage any more land than it already is responsible for.

The Ice Age Floods Institute (see sidebar) is working to educate people about the potential benefits of the trail and to encourage Congress to move the project forward. Members of IAFI encourage people who live in the Northwest to join in their efforts.

THE ICE AGE FLOODS INSTITUTE

The Ice Age Floods Institute (IAFI) is a nonprofit, volunteer-based organization committed to the recognition and presentation of the ice-age floods as a significant part of the United States', and the world's, natural heritage. The institute was incorporated in 1995 and includes among its members many amateur and professional geologists, as well as people with interests or careers in other natural sciences and fields such as education, agriculture, outdoor recreation, and community development. Writers, artists, photographers, and avid hikers are also among its members. The best way to gain some familiarity with this organization is to visit its website (www .iafi.org), which provides information about these topics:

- The immensely powerful, cataclysmic ice-age floods that swept across the Pacific Northwest during recent geologic time
- The proposal for an Ice Age Floods National Geologic Trail, which would be a system of travel routes linking significant sites and interpretive facilities across the region

The Ice Age Floods Institute is a nonprofit organization dedicated to the authoritative presentation of the fascinating but little-known story of the floods.

IAFI sponsors field trips and lectures; encourages the exchange of information among interested individuals, organizations, and agencies; and works to expand the range of interpretive resources and materials available to the public.

The IAFI online store offers the best books, maps, and DVDs available on the ice-age floods. Buying from the store supports IAFI in its mission to educate the public and increase appreciation for the floods story. The store is found at the IAFI website.

IAFI local chapters are found throughout the Northwest, from Missoula, Montana, to Portland, Oregon, and from Seattle to Spokane in Washington State. Through these local chapters, IAFI brings the story of the ice-age floods to life in local communities, especially in areas directly affected by the floods. You don't need to belong to a local chapter to be a member of IAFI, but becoming involved with a local chapter is a great way to participate in projects and activities and to build partnerships in your communities.

WHY DO WE NEED AN ICE AGE FLOODS NATIONAL GEOLOGIC TRAIL?

There are many reasons why this trail is an excellent proposal. The region lacks a coordinated interpretive approach to the ice-age floods story. The understanding and appreciation of the ice-age floods is a relatively recent phenomenon. As recently as the 1960s, not all geologists accepted the hypothesis of catastrophic ice-age flooding in the Pacific Northwest. It took decades for the geologic community to accept the hypothesis of J Harlen Bretz, who was instrumental in proposing the idea of catastrophic flooding. In 1979 the Geological Society of America awarded Bretz the Penrose Medal, the nation's highest geological award.

In 1986 John Allen and Marjorie Burns published *Cataclysms on the Columbia*, which sparked a wave of public interest in the floods. In 1994 a video of the floods was developed by the Washington State University Landscape Architecture program, in cooperation with the National Park Service, and a year later *Smithsonian* magazine featured an article by Michael Parfit on the floods. In 1998 Oregon Public Broadcasting produced a video program on the floods, and public awareness of this significant geological event increased dramatically.

During the 1980s and 1990s, tourism—especially "cultural tourism"—grew at a rapid rate in the Pacific Northwest. The income from increasing tourism helped offset economic losses that occurred in some parts of the region from reduced timber and mining activities.

The visible remnants of the floods are on such a large scale and found at so many different sites that change has not dramatically affected them, but as the area continues to develop, the region will experience accelerated changes. These changes may affect floods features. At the present time, there is an opportunity to develop a cooperative effort to educate the public about the ice-age floods; to contribute to existing cultural tourism programs in Montana, Idaho, Washington, and Oregon; and to develop a better understanding and appreciation of the remaining resources from the greatest documented floods on Earth.

WHERE THINGS STAND IN CONGRESS

In March 2009, the Ice Age Floods Trail bill passed Congress. Shortly after, President Obama signed the bill into law.

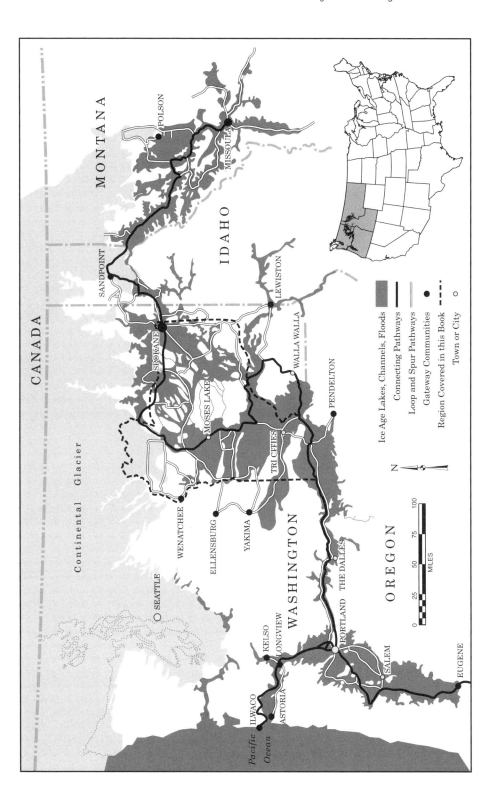

The National Park Service will now oversee the Ice Age Floods National Geologic Trail, which will cost an estimated $8 million to $12 million to establish. Appropriation of money to staff the trail and create the management plan is the next task. The process of establishing a trail such as this is often long, and appropriating funds in a bad economy will no doubt slow the process.

Perhaps the most effective argument for developing the trail is its economic benefits. By raising awareness of the ice-age floods, the trail will both encourage domestic tourism and attract international visitors. The increase in tourism could be particularly beneficial for many of the rural communities in the region.

In addition, through a partnership of many public and private participants, the proposed trail offers the opportunity to draw local economic benefit from much publicly owned land. It should be possible to act on a regionwide, nonpartisan basis to implement the trail proposal.

Decades from now, when an Ice Age Floods National Geologic Trail has been developed, tens of thousands of people will stop at various sites along the route of the floodwaters and marvel that a natural force with such fury and energy could have created the remarkable landscape of the Channeled Scablands—and all in such a brief amount of time.

The Channeled Scablands are as much a national treasure as the Grand Canyon, Yosemite, and Yellowstone. Though remarkably different from any other geological area in the United States that has been set aside for its unique natural attributes, the Channeled Scablands represent a wonderful learning laboratory for future generations to explore and enjoy.

RECOMMENDED RESOURCES

If your curiosity is piqued about the ice-age floods and geological features found in the Channeled Scablands, some additional reading and viewing will get you up to speed. A number of good books, videos, and websites will help you learn more about one of the greatest geological events to ever occur on Earth and provide more detailed trail information if you want to explore these lands more extensively yourself.

Allen, John Eliot, Marjorie Burns, and Scott Burns. *Cataclysms on the Columbia: The Great Missoula Floods.* Rev. ed. Portland, OR: Ooligan Press, 2009. This new edition of a popular book tells two stories. One follows geological research that challenged the scientific paradigm of the early twentieth century, and the other chronicles the results of that research: the discovery of the powerful prehistoric floods that shaped the Pacific Northwest.

Alt, David. *Glacial Lake Missoula and Its Humongous Floods.* Missoula, MT: Mountain Press, 2001. This narrative follows the path of the floodwaters as they raged from western Montana across the Idaho Panhandle, then scoured through eastern Washington and down the Columbia Gorge to the Pacific Ocean.

Baker, Vic. "Joseph Thomas Pardee and the Spokane Flood Controversy." *Geological Society of America Today* 5, no. 9 (September 1995). gsahist.org/gsat2/pardee.htm. Geologist Vic Baker explores geologist Joseph Pardee's involvement in the hypothesis that cataclysmic floods produced the Channeled Scablands.

Bjornstad, Bruce. *On the Trail of the Ice Age Floods: A Geological Field Guide to the Mid-Columbia Basin.* Sandpoint, ID: Keokee Books, 2006. This book explores the geologic explanation for legendary floods, explains the features they created, and guides readers to trails and tours in the Mid-Columbia Basin to witness the floods' awesome power for themselves.

Carson, Robert J., and Lawrence L. Dodd, eds. *Where the Great River Bends: A Natural and Human History of the Columbia at Wallula.* Sandpoint, ID: Keokee Books, 2009. This book highlights Wallula Gap, a National Natural Landmark in south-central Washington State where geography has defined history, marked by the narrowing of the mighty Columbia River halfway between the Rocky Mountains and the Pacific Ocean.

Foster, Tom. *Ice Age Floods* (blog). iceagefloods.blogspot.com/. This geologist's blog is a neverending source for flood-related photos, captions, and commentary. Also visit Tom's informational site: HUGEfloods.com.

Jones and Jones. *Special Resource Study.* National Park Service report, 2001. www.nps .gov/iceagefloods/. Study that led to Congress authorizing formation of the Ice Age Floods National Geologic Trail; available for download.

KidsCosmos.org. "The Channeled Scablands." www.kidscosmos.org/kid-stuff/kids-canyons -scablands.html. This children's website explores four major features of the scab- lands with maps, photographs, and USGS satellite images accompanied by a glossary of geological terms.

Landers, Rich, and Dan Hansen. *Paddle Routes of the Inland Northwest.* Seattle: Mountaineers Books, 1998. A full collection of fun floats in all sorts of riparian settings around the Inland Northwest.

Landers, Rich, and the Spokane Mountaineers. *100 Hikes in the Inland Northwest.* 2nd ed. Seattle: Mountaineers Books, 2003. Includes four hikes in the Columbia Basin area described in this book.

Montana Natural History Center. "Glacial Lake Missoula and the Ice Age Floods." www .glaciallakemissoula.org. The Montana Natural History Center offers background information on the ancient floods and photographs of their stunning impact on the geography of the northwestern United States.

Newman, Jim. *Oregon Field Guide: Missoula Floods.* Portland, OR: Oregon Public Broadcasting, 1998. A video program on the floods that first aired in 1999.

Nisbit, Jack. *Singing Grass, Burning Sage.* Seattle: The Nature Conservancy of Washington, 1999. Great photo-essay book all about the Columbia Plateau, including scablands, farmland, and two great river systems.

NOVA. *Mystery of the Megaflood: Examining the World's Most Catastrophic Flood.* Aired September 20, 2005. PBS television program. www.pbs.org/wgbh/nova/megaflood/. With the help of stunningly realistic animation, NOVA takes viewers back to the last ice age to reveal what happened when the ice dam broke, unleashing a titanic flood that swept herds of woolly mammoth and everything else into oblivion.

Parfit, Michael. "The Floods that Carved the West." *Smithsonian* magazine, April 1995.

Soennichsen, John. *Bretz's Flood: The Remarkable Story of a Rebel Geologist and the World's Greatest Flood.* Seattle: Sasquatch Books, 2008. *Bretz's Flood* brings to life the dramatic story of how the Channeled Scablands came to be and how one man persevered against the odds to change the course of geologic history.

Spring, Ira, and Harvey Manning. *55 Hikes in Central Washington.* 2nd ed. Seattle: Mountaineers Books, 1997. Includes more than a dozen hikes in the Channeled Scablands.

Symons, T. W. *Report of an Examination of the Upper Columbia River.* Washington: Government Printing Office, 1882.

———. *The Symons Report on the Upper Columbia River & the Great Plain of the Columbia.* Fairfield, WA: Ye Galleon Press, 1967. A reprint of the original publication listed above.

INDEX

Page numbers in **boldface** indicate photos; "m" following page number indicates a map.

ABOUT THE AUTHOR

John Soennichsen has more than 300 articles, essays, and short fiction to his credit. His first book, *Live! from Death Valley: Dispatches from America's Low Point,* was published in September 2005. Praise for the book included this statement by *Publisher's Weekly*: "Eloquently written, Soennichsen's book is a triumph of reportage reminiscent of McPhee."

John's second book, *Bretz's Flood*, was published in 2008. It tells the story of the maverick geologist in the 1920s whose radical theories explained the formation of a wildly rugged region of eastern Washington.

John has also written *The Chinese Exclusion Act of 1882*, the historical adventure novel *Westward Journey*, and *The Fat Detective,* a tongue-in-cheek mystery novel. All these books can be found at johnsoennichsen.weebly.com.

John's bachelor's degree in journalism is from the University of Oregon and his master of fine arts in creative writing is from Eastern Washington University. His interests include hiking and photography. He lives with his family on five acres alongside a scabland channel just outside the eastern Washington town of Cheney.